MY DOT MATTERS

REDISCOVERING FAITH BY REALIZING SELF-WORTH

MEKA REED

This book is not sponsored, paid for, associated with, or distributed by/for or on behalf of The Church of Jesus Christ of Latter-Day Saints or its subsidiaries. The author does not write on behalf of the Church or any of the Church's affiliate organizations. The Author's views are her own. Her lived experiences have been recorded in this book as she remembers them and are non-fiction.

Asterisked (*) names have been changed to protect the person's identity. Some people's names have been changed to descriptions to protect the person's identity. All actual names have been used with permission.

Please be advised this book contains writing about suicidal thoughts, self-harm, and various mental health topics

Copyright © 2023 Meka Reed

All rights reserved. This book or any portion may not be reproduced, transmitted, or stored in any manner without written permission of the author.

Disclaimer: The information in this book is provided for entertainment purposes only. All content is based on the author's opinion and does not constitute any health, medical, financial, or legal advice. The ideas, suggestions, and procedures provided in this book are not intended to be a substitute for seeking professional guidance. It is not intended to diagnose, treat, cure, or prevent any condition or disease. Seek advice from your licensed healthcare provider for any conditions or concerns you have prior to reading and completing any of the techniques described in this book. The author makes no guarantee of financial or health-related results obtained by using this book. The author assumes no responsibility and shall not be held liable or responsible for any direct or indirect losses – including, but not limited to, illness, injury, damage, liability, death, or financial loss – allegedly arising from any suggestion, use, or implementation of any information contained in this book.

Blessed be the name of our God; let us sing to his praise, yea, let us give thanks to his holy name, for he doth work righteousness forever.

Alma 26:8

CONTENTS

Dedication & Acknowledgements vii

Chapter 1   Happy Birthday 1
Chapter 2   The Countdown 27
Chapter 3   Partial Hospitalization 57
Chapter 4   My Dot 81
Chapter 5   The Book and The Church 91
Chapter 6   The Blessing 111
Chapter 7   New Friends 131
Chapter 8   COVID-19 147
Chapter 9   Divorce Imminent 163
Chapter 10 The Road to Baptism 179

Free Gift For You 201
About the Author 203

DEDICATION & ACKNOWLEDGEMENTS

I want to give a special thanks to my husband, Pocket. You are my ride-or-die, and you support me wholeheartedly throughout this adventure we call 'life' in such an amazing way. I feel really blessed to be able to call you my forever partner.

Thank you to my firstborn, Theo, whose mere existence pushes me to keep going and never quit on anything I want to do in life.

To my youngest baby girl, Jo, thank you for helping me brainstorm, supporting this project when under wraps, reading the early drafts and parts of the manuscript, and giving me the feedback I needed to remain focused.

You all motivate me to be a better person and try to do great things, even when I'm afraid, and you support me unconditionally. I love you guys so much.

Thank you to my mom, Denice, and my mother-in-law, Eileen, who have encouraged me through every project I've started and never finished. Hey, I finally finished one!

To Jake and Courtney Beatty and Eric and Trisha Ashford.

Thank you for breaking the hard things into bite-sized pieces and being gentle with us as you taught us. Mostly, thank you for being our friends.

Finally, to the young sister missionaries, Abby Bullard, Rachel Robison, Amie Squire, Sinei Tiatia, Abby Michaelis, and Demi Doane. You taught us the gospel and helped us through every step of becoming baptized. My family and I are grateful for your knowledge, wisdom, obedience, and love for us and Jesus Christ.

I love you all.

1

HAPPY BIRTHDAY

"Welcome on the mod. If you need something urgently, ask a TA." The nurse waved her hand as if presenting a TV showcase.

I followed behind her trying to keep up. "What is the mod and what is a TA?"

"The mod is the floor you're on in the ward, and the technical assistants or aides help our nurses with patients. Sit here."

Sitting on a hard chair against the wall, I surveyed the room full of patients. They shuffled about the mod with dead eyes. *They look like they're under some kind of spell. How is this helping?*

My shoelaces being ripped out of my new gym shoes brought my attention back to the present.

"These are expensive shoes." I shifted in my chair trying to cover my shoes. "I need my laces."

The TA crouched in front and reached for my shoe, groaning. "We have to take your strings so you can't use them to hurt yourself."

"I'm not gonna choke myself with my shoelaces." *It would take too long and be extremely uncomfortable. If I'm going to kill myself, I'll jump in front of traffic or out of a window to get the job done quicker.*

"I'm sorry." She motioned for me to stand up. "It's policy. It's not just for you, another patient could get your laces and hurt themselves." She pulled the drawstring out of my jogging pants.

This is crazy. I'm wearing clothes, but I feel naked. It feels like I'm losing control. I can't let myself lose control.

"My shoes won't stay on if I don't have laces."

She nodded and pulled out a pair of zip ties. "We'll put these on them so they stay on."

The lock on the metal doors of the mod buzzed, temporarily snapping patients out of their zombie-like states to see who entered. A brown-skinned man immediately glued himself to a distant wall, clutching files unable to hide his ugly Christmas sweater, and scurried across to get to the medical room as his eyes darted around.

He's keeping an eye on patients as if to make sure they won't follow him. How reassuring.

"The psychiatrist is back, let's go." The TA swiftly turned, walking towards the medical room as I scrambled to keep up, holding my jogging pants up with one hand.

My hand clutched the doorframe, and then I tiptoed into the room. My heart pounded in my ears. *What am I supposed to do?*

He didn't look up. Instead, he fired off a bunch of questions.

I didn't even follow half of that. Did I want to commit suicide? Did I feel suicidal? Seriously, when will this end?

"Step on the scale."

Stepping onto the 1950's white hospital scale, I wobbled as he slid the dial back and forth until we landed on my weight.

"You're 40 years old?" He looked at his paperwork with eyebrows raised. "You don't look that old."

Are you allowed to make personal comments like that?

"Alright, we're done. I'll see you tomorrow." He opened the door and motioned for me to leave.

The TA was waiting outside. "Okay. Let me show you where you'll sleep tonight." She walked to the other side of the mod. I followed but got cut off by the janitor rolling around a large trash can. He looked at me.

"We got a new one!" He laughed.

I scowled.

The man followed us to my room. "Don't worry, you'll get used to it."

As I approached, the chant-like muttering got louder. I peeked into the room. A young woman in scrubs sat in a chair, her eyes focused. The room smelled of urine and smashed ketchup packages. Gnats, blood, and feces smeared the walls and floors. Dishes and meal trays littered the center of the floor.

I looked around the corner through the saloon door of the bathroom. The shower head was at just below chest level. *So that no one could hang themselves, I suppose.* The toilet overflowed with paper and other stuff. In the middle of this cesspool, I spotted a pristine bed with white sheets.

"There's your bed." The TA pointed.

I swallowed my vomit as I spotted a tall, disheveled woman muttering and growling. Soaked in sweat and bodily fluids, she threw the staff around like rag dolls as two other TAs tried to herd her.

"I'm not sleeping here." I shivered, glued to my spot in the doorway.

"We have people in the room to ensure you stay safe." The TA motioned towards my bed.

I stared at the woman who would be my roommate, watching her effortlessly throw a male TA across the bed.

"I don't need any witnesses to my murder." Rubbing my head, I closed my eyes. "I'm not sleeping here." *In addition to the physical danger, it's disgusting. I could catch something just from being in this biohazard.*

"You can sleep in the common area on the couch or sleep here." The TA didn't even blink.

Looking over the common area filled with patients, I noticed no one reacted to the commotion in my room; which was only two doors down. Scattered about the couch, some watched TV while others paced. The lights shone brightly. *There's nowhere for me to sleep.*

I sighed, my skin crawling. "Fine. I'll sleep in here."

• • •

The next morning, I woke up disoriented, momentarily forgetting that I was an inpatient in a mental hospital. *That was one trippy dream.*

My roommate screamed the entire night in a psychotic re-enactment of traumatic events. The night wasn't long just because of my roommate. Every fifteen to thirty minutes security would barge in, yelling 'well check' as they flashed a light directly in my face and slammed the bathroom and bedroom doors loudly.

In case someone managed to commit suicide, they said. If someone isn't already insane, they soon will be with this kind of treatment.

But we're still alive....

After splashing water in my face, I brushed my teeth and attempted to flatten the wrinkles in the only clothes I owned in the hospital; my clothes from the day before. Stifling a yawn, I shuffled out of my room. Several patients were awake. Some waited for morning medications and others gathered near a coffee dispenser. I blindly made a beeline for the coffee.

"HAPPY BIRTHDAY!" A fellow patient jumped in front of me and began to wriggle. "Happy birthday, happy birthday, happy birthday, happy birthday!" She chirped like a three-year-old on a sugar high.

Is that some sort of strange dance?

"Thanks." I attempted to side step but she jumped right back front. We danced awkwardly towards the coffee dispenser while she continued to sing and bounce.

Don't strangle her, you'll stay here longer. It took incredible willpower not to give in to my urges. Right after I reached the coffee dispenser she noticed another person and ran off.

"Hey! I'm the queen of England!" She continued to dance

an endless game of 'I'm not touching you' with another unsuspecting patient.

My coffee tasted like water, and I used an unrinsed cup, but I was still grateful for the hot liquid. I took another sip and accidentally met the emotionless gaze of another patient. Staring at one another through lifeless eyes, we drank silently.

"They're calling for you at the medicine window." A TA popped up from behind.

Dumping my coffee down the drain, I went to take my morning medications. Swallowing the pills, I grimaced. *'You've really managed to mess up this year's birthday.'*

"Open your mouth." The doctor commanded through the plated glass. I opened my mouth for him to check that the medicine had gone down. "Okay. You can join the line for breakfast."

So this is where you go when you fail to kill yourself. Great.

We staggered along the hallway in slow motion like zombies, led by a TA. Peeking through windows of locked doors while passing, I only stopped to be let through each locked security door. The medications I took started to kick in, and they kicked in harder than normal as we rounded the corner to the cafeteria. *I think there were four doors. It feels like the doctors haven't figured out the dosage yet.*

A fragrant mix of hot bacon, coffee, old wet towels, and something stale hit me. *Can you smell lights? It smells like the heat from an overhead projector.* I saw my hands make another cup of coffee, and I stood there, lost in its darkness or rather a lack thereof. There were bubbles along the perimeter.

Is this tea? I sniffed the cup.

"What would you like?" A woman with a hairnet and gloves stood behind the hot food counter.

I looked down at the food slowly.

"You can take a plate from there." She motioned to the shelf. "Or I can give you specific items."

"Um..." Confused from the medication, I walked away without taking anything. My tray held a single cup of coffee in the center. *Where am I going? I don't recognize anyone.* Scanning the room, I wondered where to sit. My feet seemed glued to the floor for what felt like several minutes.

"Hey! Over here." A guy waved. "You're new, right?"

Unable to process, I stared back blankly.

"Our mod sits over here."

I felt myself float over to his table and sat down way too hard to be considered normal. *His face looks like he's talking to me. Is it my turn to speak? I can't follow the conversation. Everyone sounds like they're speaking underwater. Or am I hearing underwater? Are we underwater?!*

"You must be on something strong." Someone chimed in. "It takes a couple of days for them to get your dosing right." The group laughed. "Everyone here has gone through it. You'll be fine. The first day is the hardest. Just attend the groups and actually participate. That way you get the most out of this and you can go home and be with your family."

Opening and closing my mouth, I struggled to speak, but I managed to sound out the words. "How long do I have to stay?"

"Oh, it depends." A girl shrugged, tossing her hair over her shoulder. "I've been here sixteen days."

"Eight days for me so far." Someone held up their hand.

"Twenty-one days." A bearded man cleared his throat.

"But the real old head is this guy." The girl threw her arm around a guy in his early thirties, with tousled brown curls and a boyish grin. "He knows everything."

"Not everything." He laughed. "But I've been here thirty-one days."

I inhaled sharply as I clutched my chest.

His face paled as he explained quickly. "I can help you out if you feel a little lost or need someone to help you cope in here."

"I don't want to be here that long!" I started to hyperventilate. "I ... wanted ... some ... control over my life! This place ... is taking ... what little I had ... away!" I gasped for breath.

The guy with the curly hair glanced around, fidgeting with his fork. "Hey, hey, hey... Don't freak out." He lowered his voice, motioning towards the staff members strategically posted around the cafeteria. "You don't want to add more time. Chill out, participate, and *eat food*." He nodded toward my tray, holding a single cup of coffee. "You'll be outta here in no time."

I nodded and quietly drank my tea-coffee in between shaky deep breaths.

"Hey." The girl who plays with her hair smiled, grabbing my attention. "Is it true that today's your birthday?"

I nodded. *Quit reminding me.*

• • •

The walk back from the cafeteria was a blur. Feet shuffled and security doors unlocked and locked until we came to a familiar door, the one to our mod. The patient who bombarded me with happy birthdays this morning was inside.

Did she not go to breakfast? I don't remember.

She scurried towards our group as we entered.

"Welcome back! Welcome! *Did you eat breakfast?* Did you eat? *Did you eat?* Did you? *Did you?*" She spoke rapidly, switching from joyful to menacing with each question.

I pushed past her.

"Fine!" She stomped her foot, raising her voice. "Well, well. The *birthday girl* got to eat breakfast! I didn't get to eat breakfast but *she did*!" She pointed at me, stabbing the air with her finger.

I looked around. *Is the medication playing tricks on me? No one responded to her, so maybe I'm hallucinating.* At that moment, a staff member walked through the secured door, and her mood went from angry to inquisitive.

"Hi, I need to talk to you." She attached herself to the arm of the staff member as they walked past.

"That was fast." I turned towards the group.

"Yeah, she does that. You'll get used to it." The curly-haired guy shrugged.

The other patients made space for me on the couch facing the TV, and I took a seat. Behind me, an elderly lady called for help from an open door in a dark room. She wheeled into her doorway slowly, revealing a tiny skeletal frame with pale yellow skin and sunken, sharp, gray eyes. "*Help...*"

We locked eyes.

"*Help...*"

"Is anybody gonna help her?" I looked at the people sharing the couch.

"They'll get to her. They always do." Another patient waved it off.

"*Help...*"

"Somebody is coming to help you right now." A TA exited the nurses' station.

At that moment, the patient who makes unwanted announcements started again. "I wanna go to group! I wanna share my feelings!"

The TA raised her hands in a pacifying gesture. "It's not time for group right now. And you can't go."

"*Whyyyy!?* I wanna share my feelings!" She cried hysterically.

"*Help...*"

"You're on a hold, you know that! We've been over this." The TA sighed, shaking her head.

"*Help...*"

"She gets to go to the group and she's NEW!" The patient pointed at me.

The staff pursed her lips. "You're on hold, and you can't go to group until you're off."

A strained silence fell, only interrupted by calls for help from the elderly lady as the patient stared at the TA, her jaw clenched and fists balled. Suddenly, in an explosion of emotions, the patient screamed, cried, and threw paper as she stormed to her room. "I'm going to take a *shower!*" The door slammed behind her.

"*Help...*"

The TA ran over to wheel the old woman out of her room. "You wanna go to the common area, or do you wanna see the TV from here?"

"I'm fine here." She nestled into her wheelchair a few feet from her door with a hint of a smile.

"Okay." The TA ran off to deal with other patients.

As soon as the staff left, the wheelchair squeaked as she slowly wheeled back into her room, stopping just inside the threshold.

"Help..."

• • •

A short line formed at the mod doors. *Someone said that it was for group therapy.* I surveyed the surrounding area; no medical staff appeared to be close nor did they respond to the line forming. The nurses' station hummed in distraction. I stood up slowly. *Is this line really for group therapy, or are we caught in another patient's delusion?*

I approached the line, still groggy from the medication. *None of the other patients seem to notice I'm here.* They all waited, eyes fixed on the tiny windows of the mod's security door, swaying subtly.

The security door buzzed, and a disheveled man in a sweater and glasses with short, messy hair emerged. "Are you guys lined up for group?" He giggled as if it were a secret that only those in the line should hear. There were various affirmative nods and groans. He did a headcount. His eyes narrowed as he quickly glanced around. "Okay. Come with me." He held the door open.

A wave of relief cascaded over me.

The mod makes me claustrophobic. It's like a huge rectangle, with the nurses' station and common area in the center. You can't go anywhere except the main area and your room. Fresh air is only for smoke breaks, which take place in a caged area directly accessible from the mod. The door is always locked so no one can escape. We're stuck like rats in a lab.

The line came to a sudden stop, no further than ten steps from the door that we exited, and then slowly rounded the corner, revealing the group therapy room.

My heart sank.

"You're a new face." The disheveled man in glasses smiled wolfishly, leaning his back awkwardly against the doorframe. "Don't worry, nobody bites here." He whispered behind his hand, giggling.

This guy makes my skin crawl. Does he think he's funny? He's taking up too much space in the door. Why isn't he moving out of the way? Read the freaking room, man!

He mumbled something incoherent without moving his mouth.

My brows furrowed. I slid past, pressed against the doorframe as if the therapist were a contaminant, and found a seat. "How long does this last?" I turned to a group member.

They answered without making eye contact. "About an hour."

Rubbing my neck, I sighed. *I can't do this.*

● ● ●

I stared at my hands, fiddling with a dull-tipped, eraserless pencil slightly larger than a bobby pin.

All of the pencils in the box are the same as if ordered that way for uniformity. A patient can't attack someone with a tiny, dull pencil, though it's small enough to swallow if you want to commit suicide. Granted, it'll be a messy, arduously embarrassing, slow, and painful death, but it gets the job done.

Without looking, I slid the pencil into my pocket.

Grabbing another pencil, I looked at the paper given to us by the sweater man. The unremarkable room had fluorescent lighting, and the glare bounced off the paper. *It's irritating my eyes.* I quickly found a chair along the room's perimeter, right outside of the circle against a wall so I could watch everyone.

At both ends, the doors were locked. The room wasn't only padded, it was insulated. *When you talk, you can hear your voice stop as it bounces against the walls.*

"Just answer the questions on the paper, and then we'll go around the group to check in." The sweater man cleared his throat.

With my paper bent over my thigh as I wrote, my dull pencil, unable to poke a hole, kept making small dents. *I don't know why this frustrates me. The pencil can't even pierce the paper.*

Hours of sleep?

Three. No. I scribbled over that answer. *Five sounded better.*

Quality of sleep: difficult, restful, tossing and turning, and nightmares.

All of the above.

Appetite: not eating, binging, purging, decreased, or no change.

Decreased.

Are you having thoughts of harming yourself or someone else?

That mood-swinging 'Happy Birthday' patient back on the mod. I could hurt her, and I'd probably feel better. On second thought, considering how loud she is, she'd probably make a big scene.

I fidgeted with the pencil hidden in my pocket. My chest tightened as I struggled to breathe normally.

How on earth do I answer this question without getting into more trouble? The minute I'm honest, I'm doomed.

Images of me being forced to hug myself in a white straightjacket, screaming in protest, while being dragged into a closet-sized room, tortured my mind. *That's what I saw them do to a patient only hours after arriving here, minus the straightjacket. The scene was burned into my brain.*

I shuddered. *What fool would answer this question honestly? Let's just circle no.*

All the chairs in the room were occupied. Patients' ages starkly contrasted, with a big part in their twenties and another big part seniors. *I seem to be one of the few in the middle.*

Only the sound of dull pencils on paper filled the air.

One person stood out. A heavyset, burly man wearing scrubs partially blocked the door. His skin was dewy with sweat. He breathed heavily as if snoring while wide awake, sitting abnormally erect, with both hands on his knees, drumming his fingers against them.

He looks like the personification of body odor. If this were a movie, he'd definitely be the killer.

He was one of the three patients on our mod dressed in hospital scrubs.

Why? Where did he get scrubs from? Is he trying to confuse other patients?

My head hurt.

There are too many things that don't make sense. Why is he allowed to block the door? Why is he dressed like a nurse? Why did staff members dress in regular clothes like patients? Why weren't people with similar diagnoses together?

"This meeting is just a check-in." The sweater man erased scribbles from the whiteboard behind him. "We aren't going to get into anything deep right now. We'll do that when we meet for our second group in about an hour or so." He joined the circle and sat in front of the whiteboard, crossing his legs. "We're going to go around the circle, introduce ourselves, and share whatever we feel comfortable sharing from our papers". A crooked smile crept across his lips.

Is anyone else seeing this? I looked around the group.

He adjusted his glasses. "Who wants to go first?" He looked around the room, calling my name while nudging a fellow patient with his elbow. The patient glared at him. He ignored it and giggled again.

What's wrong with this guy? His words and actions don't match. They're weirdly inappropriate, but not in a way that I can prove if I tell someone.

Is he trying to make me act crazy?

The tag hanging from a lanyard around his neck marked him as a therapist.

"Ummm…" I shifted uncomfortably in my seat and stared at my paper. "I had five hours of sleep last night."

Lie.

"It was restful."

Another lie.

"There has been no change in my appetite."

Lying again.

I hesitated. *How many lies have I told in a matter of seconds? I feel horrible.* Raising my eyes from the paper, I looked at him; my heart racing. I tried to smile convincingly. "I am not suicidal."

Liar.

• • •

A little while later, I met the eyes of a young blond girl with tangled hair and blue eyes that had lost their sparkle. She stood in the doorway of a dark room adorned with stitches from old cuts, her legs scarred from the ankles to the knees and her arms up to her elbows. *A clear sign of self-harm.* Neither one of us broke eye contact.

"Hello?"

She hesitated. "Meow."

I nodded. *Of course, she meows. What else was I expecting?*

Stepping closer, she reached into her pocket and pulled out two small packets of white crackers. "Meow."

I reached out, and she dropped them into my hand. Casually,

I slid them into my pocket. *We aren't allowed to bring food from the cafeteria to the mod, so these are considered contraband.*

"Thanks." I smiled weakly. The first smile in 24 hours.

"Meow." She slowly backed into her dark room until I couldn't see her anymore.

"Hey!" A commanding male voice called out to me from the medicine window. "Come get your medication!"

I hate medication. They haven't gotten the doses right for me and I always feel like I'm in a fog flying high. I've never liked that feeling because instead of euphoria it feels like I'm going to pass out. Plus I don't even know what I'm taking.

Peering into the little white paper cup that held my pills, I examined them.

The doctor shoved another paper cup filled with water through the window. I tossed the pills into my mouth and gulped them down. Then I opened my mouth wide to prove it.

The doors at the entrance of the mod buzzed and clanged, and someone in plain clothes peeked in, hugging the door. "When I call your name, line up. You have visitors."

My son Theo will be here. He promised to visit when they took me away and said he would bring clothes for me to wear. For sure he is one of my two visitors, but I wonder who the other one is. It's too bad they only allow two people to visit.

I headed towards the door before my name was called. The medicine kicked in fast. Faster than last time. My stomach dropped.

Oh no, I don't want to see my son while high. I don't want to be high. This isn't helping, it's turning me into a zombie like the others on my mod.

Before I realized it, we passed through all the locked doors in the hall and joined a long line waiting to enter the cafeteria. The line was backed into the hall and around the corner. I was in the middle of the line, and I could see my son at a far table. I squeezed closer to the entrance, pushing into the people ahead of me. They didn't notice. The line became congested as we pushed against one another until we passed the bottleneck. Freed at last, we rushed towards our loved ones.

My sister Apriel and my son stood as I fell into their arms. Apriel's large brown eyes were red. I tried to act normal, but I could barely hold myself upright. "I'm so glad you came! I love you!" I curled up against her like a teenager in love.

She smiled. "Happy Birthday! I had balloons for you, but they wouldn't let me bring them in."

My heart melted. "It's okay. I'm just glad you're here." I took turns leaning against her and my son, barely holding myself up. As if a switch were flipped, I began to slur. "I'm so tired..."

My son examined my face. "What did they give you?"

"I don't know. Medicine. I don't like it." I leaned on his shoulder. "I love you." It felt like I was in a well, falling into darkness and only able to see a tiny bit of light. *Did Theo say something about getting me off these medications? That would be nice.* I rubbed my face against someone's shoulder, trying to snap out of it. "I'm sorry. I'm so tired... I want to sleep."

How can I return to the mod if I can barely sit upright?

I heard Apriel talking. *Something about my birthday? How I'm feeling? I don't know...* I drifted off to sleep.

• • •

Stumbling down the hall to the mod, I followed a line full of over-medicated, swaying patients. When we entered, that patient was waiting to greet us. *She always seems to be waiting to greet anyone coming through the door.*

"Welcome! Welcome!" She skipped alongside us, dancing and twirling. "*Happy birthday*! We got you a cake!" She sang while spinning in circles. Stopping abruptly, her brows furrowed and she growled at me. "*We got you a cake!*"

"Get away from the door!" A TA commanded from a distance.

She burst into tears, whining like a little kid. "I'm not doing anything!" Suddenly she shot up, tears gone. "I need my medication."

I shook my head. *Switching emotions like that has got to be exhausting.*

The floor seemed to rock back and forth beneath my feet. It took everything in me not to fall. The cat girl from earlier rubbed against my shoulder. "Meow." She looked into my eyes. *What does she want? She looks like she wants to ask me something.* I looked away.

"Hey, did you ever find out what you were on?" The guy with the curly brown hair leaned back against the couch with his arms around the shoulders of two other girls around his age. I shook my head and kept walking. At the nurses' desk, I stopped to catch my bearings.

The pregnant woman, who yelled and screamed in a deep male voice when I entered the mod, came up to the nurses' desk speaking like a toddler to the nurse. She wanted a snack. And when the nurse turned her back to get one she turned to me, put her finger in my face, and hissed. "I'm gonna kill you." Then she turned back into a toddler and ran off with her snack.

Noting the room she was sleeping in, I cracked my knuckles. *Not if I kill you first.*

Thanks to that girl making unwanted announcements, word got out that today was my birthday. All day long, it's all that the patients talked about.

The staff asked me earlier if it was true, but when I confirmed it they didn't believe me. Probably because patients say all kinds of stuff that isn't true to life but is true to them. Finally, they decided to check my file and discovered that it truly was my birthday.

After they were sure, they gathered me and all the other patients around the nurses' desk to sing the birthday song, pulling out a sheet cake with white icing.

A choir of overmedicated patients sang, slowly dragging out the words, the creepiest version of the birthday song I ever heard in my life. My skin crawled, and chills ran down my spine. They sounded like the undead rising from their graves as they moaned.

There's no way I'll ever forget this. I'm going to have nightmares for the rest of my life.

Mentally escaping, I didn't realize the song was over until I heard cheering. "The birthday girl gets the first slice!" The staff member clapped.

I shook my head. "It's okay. I want to make sure everyone else gets their cake first."

That way no one will pay attention to what I do with mine.

The staff member handed out slices to the other patients and, one by one, they got their slice and made a beeline for the common area.

I grabbed my slice and made my way to my room. *Looking for solitude could add an extra day to my stay, but at this point, I've had it with all the personalities on my mod.* I threw my cake in the trash and laid down fully clothed on the bed for the night, sighing deeply.

• • •

It had only been two days, and I was already racking my brain on how to get out.

Not every psych ward is like this one. I heard from other patients that there's a place about a half hour away that gives you your own room and meals whenever you want. It's more like being in a regular hospital than a prison. I sighed.

I would have gone there, but when the patty wagon came knocking on my door threatening to pull me out of my house kicking and screaming, I hid behind my son for protection. He convinced them that he would take me to the psych ward nearest to my house so it would be easier on him and the rest of the family. They agreed and left, probably to go grab some other unsuspecting person.

That's the last time I'll tell my primary care doctor anything about my mental health. I didn't know she would call the psych ward on me!

My brows furrowed. *These noises are annoying. My roommate is so noisy.*

She alternated between crying, moaning, and gurgling as if possessed while hovering under the covers in her bed. Since I came, she struggled like this, only stopping when injected with whatever cocktail the staff used to calm patients down.

I stared at her from my bed. *This was going to be a long night ... Again.*

• • •

Group meetings took place three times a day. I stared at my paper. *This is elementary. There's no thought-provoking material, yet everyone's eating this stuff up. How do I pretend to be better without making it look like my personality changed drastically? That would be suspicious, and 'suspicious' doesn't get me released.*

"Jesus loves you." A woman in her late fifties with salt and pepper hair and hazel eyes stared at me from across the room. She didn't blink. *Is she in a trance?* I looked away.

"Hey, Jesus loves you. Jesus loves all of us. Do you believe that Jesus loves you?"

"No."

"Well, he does. And he loves me too!"

"Good for you." I pretended to study my paper.

"Jesus loves everybody!"

"Jesus loves you so much that you're in the psych ward with me." *Point for me.*

She paused, shaking her head. "I will pray for you."

"Okay." I excused myself and was let out of the room. *I need to breathe. Too bad going back to the mod isn't allowed during group sessions.* Instead, I stood in the hallway, locked between the group room and the mod, until the session ended.

The mod security doors unlocked at the same time as the door from the room. As the rest of the patients left, I slipped into the mod before anyone from my group saw.

"Hey! How'd it go in there?" The guy with the curly brown hair asked. He had his arms around two young women this time. *I didn't realize this was a coed mod. Why didn't I notice before? Are we allowed to cuddle together here? Seems like a recipe for disaster.*

"I literally wanted to die." I groaned.

"Literally. Literally. Literally. " The brunette under his right arm parroted my words. "I like how you say it, literally."

"Remember to keep participating. If you participate, you can get out of here." He smiled.

If that's true, why aren't you participating? "What are you in here for?"

"Just depression. You?"

"I don't know." I shrugged. "I mean, I tried to commit suicide, but I don't know my diagnosis. They started pumping me full of medication right away."

"See that guy over there?" He motioned to a redhead breathing through a hole in his neck. "He drank bleach. And there's a tall crazy woman who often throws TAs around, I don't know if you met her yet. They say she killed someone in one of her episodes."

"Can we really call her crazy if all of us are in here with her?"

"I mean, we're crazy, but she's crazy-crazy." He laughed.

"I know her. She was my roommate the first night and gave off heavy killer vibes. I have a new one now, and she mostly re-enacts her past. I'm literally waiting for the part where she re-enacts a murder."

"Literally. Literally. Literally. Literally."

"Help..."

The old lady in the wheelchair waited at her door again.

"Hold on! I'll come over there and help you." The nurse called out from the nurses' station.

"She really should be in a nursing home. I think she has dementia or something." The brunette who parrots shook her head.

At that moment, the locks buzzed and the mod doors swung open. A tall, athletic, and handsome blonde boy walked in slowly, hugging himself as he followed a nurse. Everything stopped as the residents watched him go up to the nurses' desk. His eyes looked red and puffy. I excused myself and went over to him.

"Hey, how old are you?" *I forgot to introduce myself. Great. Now I sound like everyone else here making random conversation. Being in this place really does a number on you.*

"Eighteen." He hiccuped through tears.

I'm old enough to be his mom. My heart softened. "How'd you get here?"

He took a deep breath. "I came to talk to a counselor about being depressed and I guess something I said made them put me on a seventy-two-hour hold."

"Man. That sucks. That means you can't make calls or leave the mod for meals for three days."

"But I need to call my mom." He pleaded with the nurse. His eyes begged me to advocate for him.

It's no use. At best, I can soften the blow. "Hey." I tried to keep my voice soft and warm. "It'll be ok. You're eighteen, so that means you're an adult even if you're still in high school. Once you're an adult your decisions have consequences. I don't know what you told them, but your parents can't get you out of here early. I'll introduce you to the people I talk to."

He fell into my arms sobbing. His tall frame enveloped me. All I could do was hold on and rub his back.

A ferocious otherworldly growl erupted down the hall. He jumped back, eyes wide. "What's that?"

"Oh, that's Maude."

"Maude?" He peered down the hallway.

"Yeah, she's not good with people, but she comes out at night and gives the staff a hard time. Just stay out of her way so you won't get hurt."

2

THE COUNTDOWN

The cafeteria buzzed with conversations. Three mods came to the cafeteria for dinner simultaneously, but we weren't allowed to eat with a different mod. The woman who makes unwanted announcements was with us. They'd finally let her out, so she was in rare form.

"That's my boyfriend!" While waiting in line, she told anyone who would listen.

Who would date her? I couldn't help but look. He was a man of about fifty, though it was hard to guess his exact age. His weathered body was slim, with blue eyes and tanned skin.

"Hiiiii boyfriend!" She blew kisses at him.

He looked back at us and mouthed: *"I don't know her."*

She slid into the seat next to him. "See, I told you this was my boyfriend." She glared at us. Then she looked at him and tried to kiss him.

He pushed her off the chair.

I turned away to hide my laughter and filled my tray. *The coffee sucks here. It smells weird and tastes like saliva.* For the sake of appearances, I poured a cup.

"Do you believe in Jesus yet?"

Great. She's back. "I would prefer if we didn't talk about religion."

"I can't help it. I love talking about Jesus. I'm a pastor's wife."

I narrowed my eyes. *Everybody's something here.*

Unperturbed, she continued. "No, really. I genuinely am a pastor's wife, and I truly want you to build a stronger relationship with Jesus Christ."

I sighed deeply, moving my tray down the line. "I don't want to talk about Jesus."

Jesus left me hanging. That guy didn't heal this physical illness that I suffer from, even as it used up all my money and made it so that I couldn't have nice things. Jesus doesn't care about me waking up in pain for the last 40 years. Yes, I'm alive, but I want to live. I'm just surviving right now. I took a plate from the server.

"Well, I'm going to keep praying for you until you -"

"Meow." It was the cat girl again.

Nice timing. "Hey, what's up?" I smiled softly.

"Meow." She held out half of a grilled cheese sandwich.

"Are you giving that to me?"

"Meow." She fixed her eyes on mine and chewed on her long, blond hair.

I took the sandwich and put it next to my plate on the tray. "Thanks."

A smile lit up her face as she scurried away.

"I'm going to stay on you about Jesus." The pastor's wife huffed.

I ignored her, walking to the table with the curly-haired guy with depression, the girl who parrots, and the girl who meows.

Somehow they've become my people.

● ○ ●

Full from dinner, we all sat on the couch in the common area, watching TV. The news was on 24/7. *That doesn't make sense. Won't it trigger patients, especially if the channel is biased?*

I got up from the couch. *It's too soft, I'm starting to fall asleep. Can't go to sleep early, they'll say I'm antisocial.*

The hardest part about being sane in an insane environment is that everything you do as a well-balanced person can also be attributed to insanity. Things like taking alone time, taking a nap, getting upset, showering midday, coloring, reading to yourself... everything.

It feels like I have to unlock a combination lock to get out of here.

I sat on a hard chair across from the nurses' station, where I could still see the TV. Another growl erupted down the hall. Suddenly, bloodcurdling screams echoed. I stood up and stuck close to the wall, watching the corridor intently.

Maude rushed out of the room and into the hall, mumbling and growling as if possessed by a demon, her six-foot frame dragging three nurses through the hallway. One let go and tumbled onto the floor. She threw the second into the wall. The last held onto her as she rode her back.

During the commotion, a few TAs attempted to block her. She swung a left hook into the face of a TA, who crumpled onto the ground.

Intrigued by her mumbling, I didn't think to move out of the way.

The nurse next to me was grabbed by the neck and slammed onto the ground. Suddenly, her green eyes locked onto mine. "Mommy?"

"Sure honey, what are you doing? Why are you doing this?" I immediately jumped into character. *I hope her mom didn't do something traumatic to her, or she'll probably kill me.*

"He made me do it. I didn't want to do it, but he was supposed to marry me." She whined, her eyes glued to mine.

I fixed my gaze. *If I look away, she might go back on a rampage.* In my peripheral vision, I could see the nurses tending to the TA and helping each other off the floor. None of the other patients looked. Their glazed eyes stared at the TV in a drunken stupor.

"What did you do?" I reached out to touch her and then changed my mind. *I don't want to do anything that would snap her out of her current state.*

"I had to kill him, mommy. He said he was going to marry me, and he didn't. He married her. So I had to kill them and bury them under a tree."

Is that a confession?

The nurses crept up behind her with an injection.

"It's okay, baby. It's okay." I tried to comfort her as the nurses grabbed her and quickly injected the tranquilizer.

Maude freaked out. "He made me do it. Dad said I should do it. Dad raped me and made me drink bleach!" She screamed and tossed the nurses again. Some of the staff grabbed her clothes. Dragging them to the center of the mod, where everyone was watching TV, she tore them off along with her clothes while continuing to mumble.

Another nurse came with a needle and injected her. The injections weren't working. The staff banged on the medicine window and pleaded for help. The doctor inside locked the door and window and refused to come out.

I shook my head. *Pathetic. He's afraid of his own patients. Someone needs a new job.*

Maude stood there buck-naked. No undergarments at all. Her skin touched the floor as they tackled her and stuck her with the last injection they were allowed to use.

Heart pounding, I surveyed the room. All the other patients stared unblinkingly at the television, even though she slithered completely naked along the floor in front of them. I shook my head.

Now this is jaded.

• ◦ •

In the shower, I watched the warm water run off my stomach. The showerhead was positioned a little lower than chest level. *Enough to not hang myself standing or sitting. I could probably sit* down and drown in the water if desperate, but I wasn't. Besides, there's no shower curtain, and the bathroom door is saloon-style, so I'd probably get caught. I squatted, trying to wash my hair, but it only got half wet.

I just got on my knees to wet the rest of my hair when I heard someone walk into my room.

"I know you're in here!" A child's voice sang.

It's the pregnant woman from before.

"I said, I know you're in here!" She let out a low, menacing growl.

Sighing, I clenched my fist. *I can never get a moment alone in this place.* Sleep-deprived, stressed out, and overstimulated, I struggled to keep it in. *Try not to crack.*

"Get out of my room!" I yelled from the shower, cutting off the water and reaching for my towel.

She giggled, imitating me. "Get out of my room!"

She actually does a great impression of me.

"Okay." I pushed the bathroom door open forcefully. It flew open with a loud bang as I strode towards her. *I'm going to take all my frustrations out on her face, even if she's pregnant.* However, she ran out of my room right away.

I left the door open a crack and stood near my bed so that the people on the couch in the common area couldn't see me naked, and quickly dressed. *We're not even allowed to close our doors. That gets you extra time.*

The lights felt brighter than usual as everyone sat in the common area to give a recap of their day. The TA handed out sheets of paper with questions about anxiety and depression levels. The paper also asked about suicidal ideation. A new TA gave us blue pens to write with.

Blue pens? We aren't allowed to have anything but two-inch dull pencils to write with. Did anyone else notice the mistake? I looked around. Everyone wrote without pausing or even looking at each other. *Doesn't look like it.*

"I need my medicine!" The girl who makes unwanted announcements fidgeted.

The TA shook his head. "Hold on. We'll give you your medication after we finish this."

She quieted for a few minutes and continued to write.

After a few moments, the TA cleared his throat. "Okay. Who wants to share?"

The girl who makes unwanted announcements walked into the TA's personal space with her hand raised. "I want to share!"

"Okay, step back, and you can share." The TA held his arm out to make space between them.

The girl who makes unwanted announcements straightened her paper and read. "I had a good day."

"Help…"

The old lady was awake again and sat in her doorway in her wheelchair.

"I am a little bit depressed because I need my medicine." She glared at the TA.

"Help…"

The blond girl who meows peered out of her dark room. She had been in her room for a long time. *I hear that sometimes they even have to lock her out of her room to keep her out.*

"I'm not suicidal …" The girl who makes unwanted announcements continued to read. Suddenly, she burst into tears. "I need my medicine! I need my medicine!"

The TA tried to calm her down. "Hey, we give out medicine at the same time every night. It's not time yet."

She threw herself onto the couch and scribbled all over her paper. Her pen scritched loudly as she ground her teeth.

The pen will break at this rate.

He surveyed the rest of us. "Does anybody else want-"

Through angry tears, she yelled out her multiple diagnoses. "I need my medicine! I NEED MY MEDICINE!" She pulled at her clothes and picked at her skin.

"Help…"

"Calm down! You will get your medication. You just have to wait a little bit!" The TA looked flustered.

"I….NEED….MY….MEDICINE!" She jumped onto a nearby round end table.

The TA walked up to her and snatched the blue pen out of her hand forcefully. "You'll get your medicine." He motioned to the nurses' station.

Inching out of her room, the girl who meows closely observed the scene.

The nurse arrived and gave the girl who makes unwanted announcements a shot of something that calmed her. She slumped onto the couch with a smile.

I watched her with furrowed brows. *How strange. I've never seen a person with her diagnosis act that way.*

"Meow." The girl who meows slid beside me on the couch. There was no room, so she sat partially on my lap.

"*Help...*"

"We're going to help you in just a moment." The nurse reassured the old lady.

"Okay, now that everyone is situated, who wants to go next?" The TA looked around.

The overweight guy in scrubs raised his hand, the sweat making his shirt look like a wife beater. He breathed through his mouth so loudly it sounded like he was snoring. "I had a good day."

The nurse wheeled the elderly lady into the group and parked her three people down from me.

"I have a little bit of anxiety." Sweat ran down his face like shower water. "I'm not suicidal."

"Good!" The TA collected his paper. "Anyone else?"

The elderly lady raised her hand.

"Sure! Go ahead."

She lowered her hand, trembling. We stared intently as she practiced mouthing some words and clutched her shawl. "My ... um." She paused, struggling to get the words out. Then she announced something vulgar, wrapped in compound expletives.

"Ew." My mouth reacted faster than my brain could stop it. *How can something like that even come out of an elderly lady's mouth?*

● ● ●

The following week drudged by the same. *Crazy. I'm not sure I'm allowed to call it that, but it's true.* Maude got dragged off of the ward, kicking and screaming. *Someone said they saw her in police custody.*

The curly-haired guy finally went home, and so did the girl who parrots. On top of that, the parents of the eighteen-year-old kid came to pick him up, and the pregnant lady moved to another psych ward.

Things finally calmed down a bit. Though it's almost Thanksgiving, and I'm still here. I definitely don't want to be here for the holiday. I wrung my hands. *It feels like I'm racing against the clock.*

When my long-term partner Pocket and our son Theo came to visit, I begged them to talk to the therapist so that I could get released. We sat in one of the session rooms with the therapist, anxiously waiting for someone to talk first.

I glanced at my partner. *I wonder if Pocket got enough sleep. He's even paler than usual if that's even possible. Even if his red hair darkened as he got older leaving only his beard its original red, he's still practically allergic to the sun. The complete opposite of Theo and me.*

"She seems to be improving." The therapist shifted his eyes to me and mumbled something, supposedly a joke.

My son raised his eyebrows.

I don't get the joke, and it doesn't look like Theo finds it funny either.

"How long before we can take her out?" Pocket asked.

The therapist took a deep breath. "Well ... she's doing well, even though she keeps talking about going back to work." He mumbled something, elbowing the air.

My family isn't used to how weird my therapist is. He tells jokes no one understands, elbows somebody (or the air), winks, and laughs at nothing.

Both my boys narrowed their eyes.

"I think if she gets out, she absolutely must go to our outpatient program." He put his hand to his mouth as if telling a secret. "And she has to finish, or she'll have to come back here."

Dude, I can hear you.

Theo sighed. "How long is that program?"

"It depends on how well she does, but it's usually something like 8 am to 5 pm every day, including Sundays for at least two weeks." He smiled.

That's so inappropriate. What are you smiling for? I glanced over to Pocket and Theo, who sat there with jaws clenched. *Looks like my family's had enough.*

My son crossed his arms. "Can she get out before Thanksgiving?"

The therapist mumbled something to himself that we couldn't hear and then looked at us. "It really depends."

"She's got to be out by Thanksgiving." My son wasn't going to let him weasel out of it.

"We can pick her up the day before if necessary." Pocket softened the blow.

The therapist shrugged. "Yeah. That's fine. I'll see what I can do." He leaned forward, holding up his finger. "If she gets out, she can't drive or make decisions on her own."

My family stood up silently, ready to go. *Looks like this therapist can at least read the room. This conversation is over.*

The therapist stood up too, and let us out of the session room.

I hugged both of my guys, taking a deep breath of their cologne, savoring the moment. *It feels like this is the last time I'll ever see them.* I watched them go through the first set of locked doors. The lock buzzed metallically and clanged behind them as it shut.

Don't cry. Don't cry. Don't cry.

I tried to keep my head down as tears welled up in my eyes. *It feels like I'm trapped.* I made a beeline to my room. *I need an excuse to be here. One that doesn't mean I'm feeling emotions that could push back my release date.*

Stripping my clothes off, I rushed to the bathroom and hastily jumped into the shower. Dropping onto my knees, I sobbed desperately and quietly, letting the water run over my head. *I've reached my breaking point, but I need to pretend to be okay if I want to get out of here.*

"Hey, are you okay in there?" It was the voice of one of the nurses.

Choking back hiccups, I let water run over my face. "Yeah, I'm just taking a shower." I sang back in a forced chipper voice.

The nurse's footsteps came closer, and I knew she could see me through the saloon door. Quickly I moved my hands as if washing my hair.

"Okay…Wrap it up. It's almost time for dinner."

"Mmmhmmm." I cut off the water, facing away from her so she couldn't see the front of my naked body, and waited until her footsteps grew faint. I quickly glanced toward the door while grabbing my towel. Salty tears ran down my face, mingling with shower water, and I buried my face into the rough fabric.

Keep it together, and you'll be out of here. Just keep it together.

Hovering around the nurses' station, I spoke to them cheerfully as I do every so often. *It's nice to have a normal conversation, one that reminds me of being on the outside. Maybe it's because I hang around so much, but some nurses seem to forget that I'm a patient. I hear a lot of information that I shouldn't this way.*

The mod doors flew open. and a petite woman in her late forties appeared, clutching her belongings.

It's a familiar look. Everyone has that look when they first get here unless they're in active psychosis. Most come in hugging the wall, as if everyone on the mod is contaminated.

Her cheeks were wet with tears. "I don't belong here! My husband and kids don't even know I came here!" She cried frantically, pleading with the nurses.

Wow. They're acting like she's invisible. Nobody acknowledged her pleas. I suppose, in this line of work, you see people begging to get out all the time, so it doesn't faze you anymore.

"It's three days before Thanksgiving! My family is coming in from out of town." She sobbed. "I left to go to the grocery store and never came back. They're going to think something happened to me!"

Technically, something did happen to her. She managed to get herself locked up in the mod on a seventy-two-hour hold. That means no calls, visitors, or leaving the mod for three days.

She grabbed me by the arm. "You look normal…"

What?

"I came here to get some advice." Her grip tightened. "I just needed someone to talk to. I was feeling a little depressed…" She groaned.

"How'd you get in here then?" I looked at her with less compassion than I should have for someone in her situation.

Wiping her face, she shook her head, squeezing her eyes shut briefly. "I went in there to explain how I felt… Okay, maybe I embellished a little bit…"

There it is. A small smirk danced across my lips as I shook my head.

"I thought they would give me a referral somewhere, and then that would be it. The next thing I know, they're telling me I have to stay. I told them I couldn't stay. When I got up to leave, they grabbed me, claiming that I was resisting, and they put me on a hold!" She broke down in tears again.

If there's one thing I could change about the psych ward, it would be how quickly they throw people in there. They keep a person for anything, especially if you come to get help alone.

Those who refuse get put on a hold and dragged to the mod anyway. Those who fight or protest get tagged with some defiance disorder and kept longer. It's easy to see how perfectly healthy people could end up in this place with a diagnosis.

"I wish there was something I could do, but I'm in here just like you, doing my time." I shrugged helplessly.

"YOU DON'T KNOW WHO MY HUSBAND IS!" She erupted, raging against the nurses at the station. "This is a violation of my rights!"

I mean, she isn't lying. It does feel like your rights are violated here.

"Jesus loves you!" The preacher's wife made her way over to the distraught lady.

"Now is not the time." I shushed her.

"I'll have this WHOLE PLACE shut down! You wait and see!" She waved her fist. "NOBODY will have a job when I'm through with this place!"

Uh-oh.

I can see it in the face of one of the nurses. This new lady would soon earn herself one of those calming injections. I don't know what they put in it, but it takes the fight out of whoever they give it to.

The lady continued her tantrum. "Let me use the phone! I'm calling my husband! I'm getting out of this crazy house! I don't belong h-" She slumped into the arms of a nurse like a toy that had its batteries taken out. Her eyes looked at me with betrayal.

I don't know why she's looking at me like that. She earned herself that injection.

"Jesus loves you. I just want you to know…" The preacher's wife prattled on to the woman, who now looked like she was high off the medication.

"I don't want to be here." She slurred her words while being led to the couch in the common area.

Nobody actually wants to be here.

The preacher's wife turned to me. "Do you love Jesus yet? Do you believe it?"

This lady really needs to work on her proselytizing skills.

"If I believe Jesus loves me, will you leave me alone?"

She looked into my eyes, paused, then pursed her lips and shook her head. "I'll pray for you."

It sounded more like a threat than a promise. *Great.*

● ● ●

Nothing like an early morning stretch in my doorway at the crack of dawn. The door next to mine opened a little wider, revealing the girl who meowed. Her eyes seemed to pierce through me as she held a tendril of wavy blond hair between scarred fingers. Her sleeveless shirt revealed red horizontal scars from her wrist to her elbows.

I smiled. Despite being the only one left from my original group of friends, she had been hiding a lot in her dark room lately. *Thinking about it, she behaves like a cat too. Whenever we're near each other, she rubs up against me as she passes. Skittish around people, she communicates by meowing.*

"Do you want to see what I have?" A voice whispered.

Hiding my surprise, I turned to look at the girl who meowed. *I don't want her to run off now that I know she can actually talk, so I've got to speak as calmly as possible.* "What is it?"

She opened her hand slowly, revealing a handwritten letter, folded down to about two inches so it was small enough to hide.

I gasped. "Awwww ... contraband!" Smiling, I winked.

She nodded, her eyes lighting up. Reaching into her pocket, she slipped two white crackers into my hand while whispering. "Contraband."

"You're up early." A TA interrupted.

The girl who meows scurried back into her room, and I slid the crackers into my pocket. "Yeah, I guess I'm just hungry. I didn't like dinner yesterday." I walked into the main room. *Dinner wasn't all bad, but they didn't need to know that.*

"There's fresh coffee if you want some." The TA stayed close.

I nodded and strode over to the coffee station. The fluorescent lights hummed. *This is my first time hearing them. I'm not used to it being so quiet. And I've never had the couch to myself either. The common area feels large and empty.* The nurses' voices echoed through the mod from the station.

The woman in her late forties was leaving early. Her face contorting in anger, she seethed. *Her husband must be some bigwig, after all. That's the only way someone could get out of a three-day hold before the time was up. I'd love to know what the secret is.* The staff led her away. The locks buzzed as the doors opened to release her into the double-locked hallway.

Someone cleared their throat.

The guy in medical scrubs stared at me; sweat beads suspended across his brow like tightrope walkers. "I used to own my own business."

I stared at my coffee cup, watching him from the corner of my eye. *Where did he come from? If I ignore him, will he go away? His hands look like they'd be clammy. He'd better not try anything. Ugh!*

"I've always had very good jobs - CEO, CFO ... stuff like that. I just had a bit of a breakdown."

I nodded.

"I've noticed many people here have not been in my position. They don't have the education or experience."

He had my attention. *I feel the same.*

"I feel like you are different. I've been watching you…"

I know.

"You probably haven't noticed, but I have. When we get out of here, we should keep in touch." He offered.

"Yeah … maybe. When we get to the outpatient program, give me one of your business cards." I sipped on my coffee.

He nodded in agreement, but he never looked away.

This conversation is clearly over, in my opinion. My coffee was suddenly the most interesting thing I ever saw in my life, anything to not have to look at him.

"You know, you look different than the others in here."

Is it because I'm the only black person on this mod?

"You are pretty. Like one of those people you would see on TV." He kept going. "You don't look like you belong here."

I smiled tightly. "Yet, here I am."

He nodded, and we both sat in silence with the TV turned off. I drank my coffee, and he stared at me.

"Did the old lady die?" The preacher's wife was awake and crept up behind me.

"I don't know. I haven't seen her." I turned to look at the door belonging to the elderly lady.

"I went into her room, and the bed was made. She was gone."

The preacher's wife made a cross. "So I thought maybe she had died."

The girl who makes unwanted announcements approached the common area with her coffee.

"Close your door when you leave your room, she steals stuff." The preacher's wife nodded in the girl's direction.

"How can we close our doors?" I rolled my eyes.

"I don't know, but she's a thief and a drug addict." The preacher's wife hissed as she quickly sat on the couch.

A hush fell over the common area as the girl who makes unwanted announcements plopped down in a nearby chair. "I know you guys are talking about me."

Everyone acted as though they didn't hear her.

Two more days, and I'm out of here.

• • •

I sat in a group session loopy from the medication, daydreaming about going home.

It's amazing how easily someone can take everyday things for granted. Stuff like a cell phone, shoelaces, writing utensils, and food you take to bed become contraband in the psych ward. A need for peace displays antisocial behavior and can get three extra days tacked on to your stay.

As hard as it was to snap out of it, I surveyed the room to see if anyone was feeling the same. Zombified faces staring mostly at the floor proved that I wasn't the only one feeling out of it.

"Does anyone want to share?" The therapist glanced at each patient. Then he nominated the girl who meows.

She sat quietly on a chair, knees folded against her chest, staring at the therapist. The silence went on until it became uncomfortable for everyone.

"Are you going to share?"

She hissed at him like a cat and threw her pencil at him.

That set off the girl who makes unwanted announcements. "Let me out of here. I can't breathe!" She stood in the center of the small session room, taking up more space than necessary.

"I'd like everybody to calm down." The therapist tried to de-escalate.

"Everybody? She's the only one standing." The new guy, a short man appearing to be in his fifties with salt and pepper hair, slurred his words.

"I don't want to be here anymore!" She pulled at the locked door. "I need my medicine!"

We just had our medicine before the session. Maybe she IS a drug addict.

"Okay. Okay. Okay... let's calm down." The therapist elbowed the guy who sweats a lot. He brought his voice down to a whisper. "Let me get a TA, and we can get you back on the mod." He quickly slipped out of the room.

As if a switch flipped, the girl who makes unwanted announcements sat calmly on her chair, waiting for the therapist to return.

Moments later, keys rattled and the door flew open. The therapist quickly entered the room, followed by two nurses, to discover the girl who was hysteric sitting quietly and unmoving. They looked at the therapist pointedly as they motioned for her to come with them. She stood up calmly, silently following them out.

The preacher's wife, with raised eyebrows, nodded towards me knowingly.

The therapist shook his head, sighing deeply. Then he bit his lip, fidgeting on his chair, and looked around the room. "Okay. Who would like to go next?"

● ● ●

The girl who meows, the new guy, and I sat at the lunch table, glancing at one another as we ate silently.

Meal times became awkward ever since the curly-haired guy got out. This new guy is very defensive. He regularly accuses people of saying or implying offensive things that they didn't mean or say. Why is he even sitting with us? The girl who meows and I never talk at meal times, but we trade shy smiles to show we enjoy one another's company. It's nice.

"Can I sit with you guys?" Nails black with dirt clutched a tray tightly.

My stomach lurched. "Yeah …" I swallowed. *The guy who sweats seems to consider us friends after our conversation earlier. I hope he doesn't stink.*

He sat down with a big smile in the empty chair next to me, humming and snoring as he breathed. As he sat, a whiff of body odor, musty skin, and sweat assaulted me.

Based on the smell, I'd reckon he wore the same medical scrubs the whole time I was on the mod. I smiled tightly. *Be nice. Be nice. Be nice.*

"So, what have you been up to?" Mentally, I face-palmed myself. *What else would he do in this place? Everyone does the same thing here.*

"I talked to my family on the phone today. They said they might visit me tonight." He grinned.

I feel bad for him. My family comes every night, but I'm the only one in the mod to receive such devotion. Seven o'clock in the evening is the highlight of my every day. I wouldn't have survived this far without those visits.

Fidgeting with my fork, I bit my lip. "Have they visited before?"

"No. It's the first time my wife might come to visit. I've basically just been here on my own." He shoved a mouthful of food into his mouth. "I brought myself here and got checked in. Every time I call, nobody answers the phone, so I'm happy that I finally got in touch with someone."

"That's good. Here's hoping that she can come." I pushed the food around on my tray.

"Guyyys." The preacher's wife singsonged. "Have you found Jesus yet? I've been praying for you all." She slid into the seat next to the new guy and made eye contact with me.

"I don't believe in God." The sweaty guy in medical scrubs scoffed. "I'm an atheist."

The girl who meows nodded her head.

Here we go again. I shook my head. "I know who Jesus is. He's not lost, so I don't need to find him. We're just not on speaking terms right now."

"Oh, I love Jesus so much! I wouldn't be here without him…"

Can't she give it a rest? I'm leaving. Sighing loudly, I grabbed my tray.

She leaned over the table to grab my wrist. "I'm not kidding when I say Jesus loves you."

"It's complicated. I can't say he's not there, but I can say that he sure doesn't know that I exist." I pulled my wrist free and made my way to the trash can. After coming to the psych ward, my appetite had been slim to none. *If it wasn't the medication, it was the conversation that ruined my appetite.*

I headed to the coffee station. *At this point, I almost appreciate the watered-down hot spit they give us.*

"My boyfriend is over there." The girl who makes unwanted announcements repeated it to anyone unlucky enough to be nearby. She pointed to the guy from last time and ran over to sit at his table.

The alleged boyfriend squirmed in her tight hold. She tried to kiss him, and he dodged. He wrestled out of her embrace, holding both of her arms out so she couldn't hug him again.

Anywhere else, this would be sexual assault. He didn't push her this time though. This train wreck of a one-sided relationship is making me uncomfortable. I turned away, coming face to face with an athletic, angry, bald guy.

"Were you staring at me?" His voice was gruff as he furrowed his eyebrows.

"No." I started walking towards my table.

He grabbed me by the shoulder and spun me around. "I SAW you looking at me!"

Knocking his hand off of my shoulder, I sighed. "I said I

wasn't looking at you!" *This is it. This guy is going to get me tacked with defiant behavior and delay my release.*

He squared up with his fists balled. "Don't be looking at me!"

I narrowed my eyes and balled my fists as well. *This is my first time seeing you, and I'd like it to be the last.* "Bruh, I don't even know who you ARE!"

"Cut it out before I kick you two out of here!" The lunch lady waved her ladle from next to the coffee station.

He backed away slowly, maintaining eye contact with me through furrowed brows.

The lunch lady placed a hand on her hip, still swinging the ladle. "I mean it!"

"If I see you again…" He hissed at me, giving me the finger.

Rolling my eyes, I made my way back to my table. *How hard can it be to have one day without drama, random outbursts, or hearing about Jesus? I just want to get out of here.*

• • •

After eating hours, the cafeteria became the meeting place for family members and patients. *At least during visits, family members can bring clean clothing for their loved ones in the psych ward.* While my new set of clothes was examined for any harmful items or contraband, my family and I caught up.

These guys are my world. Patients can only choose four people to visit them during their entire stay, with two visitors per night. That's why I only wrote down family members who I know will come every day. With such limited access, I can't afford to choose someone who won't be able to make it.

A phone beeped, interrupting my thoughts.

Thankfully, I left my phone with Theo. He's been answering all my text messages so that nobody would know that I was locked up.

As my son briefed me on the conversations he had under the guise of being me, a woman screamed out. *Hmm, I'd diagnose that as 'agonized disbelief'.*

"You put me in here! You did this to me!"

A hush fell over the room. Her family member whispered something to her, but we couldn't make out what he said. *I wonder what happened. Looks like everyone else wants to know as well.*

"I can't believe you'd do this to me!" She attached a string of swear words. Standing up so quickly that her chair wobbled dangerously, tears ran down her face.

Someone's about to have a nervous breakdown.

"You stuck me in here to be with HER!? You are MY husband. You're supposed to protect me!" She swung her fist at him, connecting with the top of his head as he ducked. "Get me out of here! Get me out!"

He did that on purpose, didn't he?

That guy provoked her, knowing she would react that way, so the staff would carry her away and put her on a hold. She'll have no recourse. While these are normal emotions for someone experiencing major betrayal, I've been here long enough to know that showing any big emotions, even if warranted, will make them sedate you and lock you up as a threat to yourself and others. This woman just orchestrated her own downfall.

Though, I can't say I'd react any differently if I were her.

The staff quickly swooped in to take control of the situation, grabbing her by all four limbs to carry her out.

"GET ME OUT OF HERE!" She spat in her husband's direction. "You won't get away with doing this to me!" She kicked and screamed while cussing out her husband as the staff carried her out of the cafeteria. Her voice faded as she went further down the hallway until it completely disappeared.

Everyone in the cafeteria stared at the husband, who straightened his shirt and remained seated alone at his table. *He has to stay there until visiting time is over because it's policy.*

I turned back to my family who raised their eyebrows and curved their lips. *They look like they're trying not to laugh.* "So, yeah... That's how things usually go in here."

• • •

Hanging around the nurses' station, I wrung my hands. *I'm so nervous. I can't even pace because it might be misinterpreted. Tomorrow I'll be released, and I don't want to do anything to extend my stay. The last thing I need is someone talking to me or pushing any emotional buttons. If I could just stay away from the other patients ...*

"Hey, I heard you're getting out tomorrow." The preacher's wife came over.

"You're leaving?" The girl who makes unwanted announcements joined in.

Whatever happened to HIPPA? I never told anyone when I was leaving. "Yep." I tried to contain my excitement.

"I want you to know that I will still be praying for you, even after you leave."

This is the least antagonistic statement she has ever said to me concerning religion. Maybe she's on good behavior because I'm so close to the nurses' station.

"Okay." *At this point, it doesn't matter anymore. I'm getting out of here.*

"YOU'RE getting out of here?" The girl who makes unwanted announcements interrupted again.

I nodded.

"You're not allowed to get out before me!" She pouted. "You came here after me!"

I glanced at the on-duty nurse, gesturing for her to lower her voice.

The janitor's cart rattled down the hallway. He looked me up and down. "Oh, so you're getting out?"

"BEFORE ME!" The girl who makes unwanted announcements huffed.

"Don't worry." He smirked. "She'll be back. They always come back."

"Not me." I crossed my arms. "I'm never coming to this psych ward again."

He laughed, wheeling away. "That's what they all say."

I ground my teeth. *Is this the way they treat all patients when they leave? I would never!*

"Remember that Jesus loves you. I was sent here to tell you that." The preacher's wife put her hand on my arm.

You were sent here because you have mental health issues. "Got it." I nodded.

The metal doors of the mod buzzed and clanged. A shockingly young-looking girl was dragged in kicking and fighting. She grabbed a nearby cup of juice and threw it on another patient.

She just got here and she's already making enemies.

The victim stood up and tried to grab her while she was being wrangled away, but missed. They sat back on the couch, frowning.

There was a small hall the size of two coat closets leading to a room barely fitting a mattress the size of a toddler bed. The mattress on the floor didn't have any sheets. *I bet it hasn't been cleaned or sanitized since Maude was in there.*

They threw her in and shut the door, which locked automatically. She pressed her face against the window, screaming and banging on the door.

"She's definitely going to be on hold." The preacher's wife whispered, slipping away.

"I'm going to go take a shower!" The girl who makes unwanted announcements ran off, leaving me alone at the nurses' station.

What do I do now? I guess I'll go to my room. Before I crossed the threshold, the girl who meows popped her head out of her doorway.

"Meow."

I smiled. *It's good to see her.* "Hey, I'm leaving tomorrow."

She stiffened and lowered her head as she held out her hand, revealing two white crackers. "Contraband."

Glancing around, I took the crackers and slid them into my pocket. "I'll be in the outpatient program after I get out." Pausing, I looked deep into her eyes. "When you get out, come find me."

"Meow."

"I would give you my social media information, but we're not allowed to keep those little pencils, and we don't have paper. Well, to be honest, I took a pencil but I lost it somewhere trying to hide it."

She motioned for me to follow her into her room.

Her darkened room, lit only by the bathroom light, was in disarray. She walked over to the desk next to a locked window and opened a small drawer revealing candy, crackers, dried fruits, and pens.

"Wow! You really DO have contraband."

"Meow." She pulled out a pen and extended her arm.

"You want me to write it here?"

She nodded, smiling proudly.

Ok..." I picked a spot on her biceps away from the scars on her arm, and out of view from the staff. "There." I handed her the pen. "Now let's get out of here before I get caught."

She's the only one I'll miss in this place.

3

PARTIAL HOSPITALIZATION

Eyes blurry, room spinning, and head splitting with pain, I laid my head on Pocket's shoulder. *Out of the psych ward for an hour, and I can't even enjoy it because I feel awful. Must have breathed in too much fresh air.*

As his family chatted around his grandmother's kitchen table, I fought to stay awake, each blink lasting longer than the last. "I don't feel good." I whined softly. *Am I going to throw up? Can I even make it to the bathroom before I do?*

I forced myself to swallow.

Pocket's shoulder vibrated as he spoke. "Can I have something for the pain?

Suddenly, two pills appeared. After I took them, I closed my eyes, and my mind drifted.

Luckily nobody knows what's wrong with me except Pocket's mom and aunt. I can trust them not to tell anyone. I massaged my temple. *I don't know if I'm ready for people to know about my mental health yet. What if they judge me?*

In the distance, I heard a soft voice. "Take her home and let her get some rest."

Pocket's shoulder moved beneath my head. He helped me stand. *I guess he decided to take me home.*

"I hope you feel better." Someone spoke, but I could no longer tell who.

The door shut behind me, and somehow I got into the passenger seat. Leaning against the cool window, I drifted off to sleep.

• • •

The next day I stood in the lobby, filled with fellow patients also there for the first day of the Partial Hospitalization program. I inhaled deeply. *Eight hours a day and seven days a week? I don't know if I'm cut out for this.*

The familiar smell of the psych ward greeted me.

No one told me how quickly I'd become used to staying in the psych ward. Being outside was stressful and difficult. I didn't realize how long I pretended to be okay until I stayed with people with issues too, and then returned to my old life. The experience changed me, and now I can no longer lie to myself. Looking around the lobby, I tried to find an open seat.

On the mod, I kept pretending to be well to get out, but the bar was low. It's easy to pretend you're not in the middle of a psychotic break. But now I have to do more than prove I'm not insane, I have to present the image of a reliable person who has everything together. My friends and family have to think I'm safe to be around their kids, loved ones, and themselves. I sighed, noticing that every seat was filled.

Many people don't understand mental illness.

The news distorts the image of mental illness by showing the worst possible examples to get ratings. Because of this, those who are sick suffer silence, afraid to come clean and get help. I spotted the coffee station.

Although some patients on the mod threatened me, the only potentially real danger was Maude, and even that wasn't guaranteed.

Most people with mental health issues think about harming themselves, not others.

Weaving through the crowd, my goal was to get a cup of coffee in my hands as fast as possible. *Anything that keeps me from standing awkwardly against the wall waiting for group therapy to start is good by me.*

"This coffee tastes horrible." A skinny guy standing next to me grimaced. His hand trembled continuously, nearly spilling the liquid.

Pouring a cup, I took a sip. "Yep. Still tastes like hot spit."

"Well, especially if you drink it straight like that." He raised his eyebrows.

I shrugged. "It does the job."

"New people come to my class!" A short, blond, mid-forty-year-old woman in a miniskirt and thigh-high heels held up her hand. Chunky jewelry, gold, silver, and diamonds adorned her neck. The bangles on her wrists clinked as she motioned to an open classroom door.

Half of the people in the lobby filed inside, including me. The small chairs proved to be as hard as they looked.

A low buzz of conversation filled the room. Everyone was freshly released from different mods in the psych ward. I surveyed the room. *Maybe I can find someone with a similar diagnosis to mine - whatever it is.*

The instructor cleared her throat. Her brightly colored nails were adorned with cubic zirconium, and her fingers with massive statement jewelry. "Hello, everyone. I'll be in charge of this class. A little bit about me, my boyfriend and I have been living together for fifteen years, and we have two kids. We just never wanted to get married, so that's why there's no wedding ring!" She chuckled.

The awkward silence that followed didn't deter her. She handed out a worksheet. "I think we should open up by getting to know each other. I'll give you a minute to fill out the worksheet, and then we can share some things you might want to share from it."

Groans echoed throughout the room.

Looking it over, I rolled my eyes. *It's the same one we went over on the mod every day. This feels so basic, like team building at a company meeting.* I zipped through the answers by rote.

If I write anything implying high anxiety, depression, or suicidal ideation, I'll be sent back to the mod. No need to lie, I'll just avoid sharing my true feelings.

Hardly a minute into the worksheet, she cleared her throat. "Okay, who wants to go first?"

There was a pregnant pause until she decided to change her approach. "Why don't we go from one side of the circle to the other?" She nodded towards a heavyset woman with bright purple lipstick wearing a moo moo, or was it a duster? It was a one-piece without buttons, a very flowing outfit. The lady flipped her braids over her shoulder and puffed up her chest as she read her entire paper.

I zoned out as several people read their papers out loud, tracing the lines on the floor with my eyes.

Suddenly, an extremely loud girl laughed. She had two braids, and her feet propped up on an empty chair. Her voice bounced off the walls as she spoke.

"I am bipolar. My roommate is giving me so many problems. She eats the food in the fridge with my name on it, and I hear her talking about me on the phone… She thinks I want her boyfriend. Actually, HE's been after me…"

I cringed. She spoke loudly and extremely fast without stopping to catch her breath. *Her voice irritates me.*

Her behavior was contagious as everyone started speaking at once, calling out their diagnosis and interjecting to share their life stories in a competition of 'woe is me'.

I don't even know my diagnosis.

"Okay, everyone." The instructor signaled for silence with her jeweled hands. "Let's do a meditation exercise, and we can get back to this after."

The room quieted. "Let's take five deep breaths." She inhaled deeply. "Inhale…. Exhale…." She guided us until we got to five. "Now keep your eyes closed and listen to your breath as you inhale and exhale for three minutes."

I couldn't focus. My mind hummed. Thoughts of my past. Things I should and shouldn't have done. Secrets. Something from kindergarten. I shook my head, trying to refocus on my breath.

This is torture.

I tried to think about a song that my grandma always made me sing as a little girl whenever I needed comfort.

Oh yeah… It's about Jesus. I shuddered.

My mind instantly went back to the preacher's wife. I shook my head again. *There has got to be a way to shut my brain off!*

"Open your eyes slowly." The instructor inhaled and exhaled one final time.

My eyes shot open, and my heart pounded a thousand miles an hour. I kept my eyes on the floor.

"Did that help anyone? Do you feel more relaxed?" She surveyed the class.

Shaking my head, I continued to stare at the ground.

She noticed. "Do you know why it wasn't relaxing for you?"

I shrugged. "It just wasn't."

"Well, maybe if you try it a few more times and get accustomed to it, you'll feel better." She turned her attention to the rest of the class. "It's okay if it didn't work for you. Different things work for different people. One of the things we'll be doing is helping you find out what coping skills work for you."

I focused on a particular line on the floor until my vision

doubled as she went around the class to get people to share what was on their paper. My name was called.

"Do you want to share what you've written?"

I looked at my paper. "Um... I'm not having feelings of suicide."

"Okay...?"

"I'm not depressed, and I only feel a little bit of anxiety." I managed to finish.

Perched on her desk, she leaned forward. "Do you know what's causing the anxiety?"

Trying to stay out of the psych ward. "I'm not sure."

She looked into my eyes as if looking into my soul. I didn't break eye contact.

"We can work on what triggers you and figure out what to do when you feel strong emotions." Her jewelry jingled as she turned away.

This is going to be harder than I thought. If I could wipe my brow in relief, I would. Instead, I nodded and tried to look content.

The problem with the Partial Hospitalization program is that I need to attend during what would normally be work hours. I already missed so many work opportunities, now I'm required to miss even more. How do people do it? How can people take this much time off work and still have a job to return to? I furrowed my brows.

Many others in the group are anxious as well. How can you stay sane when the program itself causes mental health problems? I get why people end up in the psych ward over and over again.

It almost feels like a scheme to keep people inside.

Some people use up all their vacation time in this place or one of its programs. Once they run out of money or insurance and/or lose their job, they're "graduated out" of the program leaving them in dire straits mentally, without money, and sometimes even homeless. Opening and closing my fists so that I could feel my nails poking my palms, I stared at the lines on the floor.

On top of that, they look irresponsible to friends and loved ones, causing their loved ones to give up on them because it looks like the mentally ill person is lazy or not trying to get better.

All of this causes a crisis, and they return to the mod to start from scratch. I felt my temper rising as heat seared up my neck.

It's heinous. Many people on the outside don't understand how strong a person has to be to get help and how much support they truly need.

You're caught between getting help for your mental health and keeping a job and a place to live. If you manage to keep your job, you're in deficit, and you need tons of financial support from family and friends. Inhaling deeply, I attempted to meditate like I had been taught.

People who have never experienced it don't understand that the crisis is not over when you get out.

It continues until you catch up with everything financially or get back on your feet while also being able to afford medication. Luckily, I have my son and Pocket to fill in the gaps financially while I tend to my mental health.

Most of the people there don't have the same support.

• • •

Glancing at my watch, I looked around for a single-person bathroom. *It's time to take my medication. Normally, such a thing wouldn't be a big deal, but in the program the smell of pills or the sound of the bottle opening and closing risk triggering the people around you. They were adamant about us not telling others what medication we take and never taking medication from someone else.*

After finishing my business, I headed outside to get some air.

"Do you have any Ativan?" A girl with blond hair and pink tips popped into view as I stood outside of the building, her pupils dilated.

"I mean, yeah, but I can't give it to you." I attempted to walk past. *Right, I forgot I'm not supposed to tell others what medications I take.*

"Can I get some?"

"I would but ..." I looked around. *Can any of the staff see me?* "Nah. I can't." *If I'm busted, they'll cut me off. Why would I risk that for someone I don't even know?*

She pouted. "Just ten, that's all I need."

"That's okay." I tried to push past her again.

Grabbing my arm, she clung to it. "How many do you have? Just five. That's all I really need."

"I'm sorry, I can't." I tried to let her down gently. Grabbing the entrance door, I pulled myself free. *Is she in the mental health program or the addiction program next door?*

"Okay, two! Two is all I need, and I won't ask you for anything else. I promise." She clasped her hands together as if praying.

Okay, yeah. She's in the addiction program. "Ask the psychiatrist. He'll give you some."

"I don't have him. I have that woman, and she doesn't write prescriptions like that. She says it's addictive."

I felt bad for her, even if she was jonesing. Withdrawal hurts and is stressful on the body and mind. "I can't help you with this cuz if you get hooked, I'm going to have that on my conscience. Plus someone could find out, and we both would get kicked out, or worse, end up back on the mod." *Why am I even entertaining this?*

She gave me a puppy-dog look. "I won't tell anyone."

I hesitated. "Let's switch contact info, and if we happen to see each other outside of the ward, nobody can say anything."

She nodded and hastily scribbled her info on a torn paper from her pocket. "Thanks so much!" She smiled.

"Right. Don't thank me yet." I entered the building without her. *Great. I've broken two rules in under two minutes.*

• • •

I sat quietly in the room before class, listening to the hoarse whistle of the tracheostomy hole of the red-headed guy across the room and the soft buzz of the fluorescent lights. *It's only the two of us here.*

"Hey." Air escaped as he spoke. "Is this your first day?"

Is he making conversation because he feels uncomfortable with the silence? "No, I think this is my fourth." I tried, unsuccessfully, not to look directly at the hole.

He noticed. "I got this after chugging bleach."

"Wow." My eyes widened.

"I was at my grandma's house, and they say that I came out

of the back room, said 'Hey everybody, watch this', and chugged the bottle."

"That's wild." I wrung my hands. "Did it hurt?"

"I don't know. I kept drinking until I started choking and passed out." He chuckled. The air pulsated through the hole. "What are you here for?"

"Nothing as exciting as you." I laughed. "I tried to kill myself, but after talking to you, I realize I was thinking small. Maybe I should have been more creative."

He smiled. "Funny thing is I wasn't trying to kill myself. When I have a manic episode, I do dangerous things and don't really consider the consequences. I can't consider the consequences. It's like I get ideas and just do them, but I don't always remember what I've done."

"I get that." I nodded. "I'm sort of the same. Except not as severe."

We quieted, both looking at the door.

"Is this your first time here? Were you on the mod?" *Remember to make eye contact.*

"I was on the mod for a few days. I think I saw you around, but I'm not sure. They had me on hard stuff."

"Me too." I fought back the urge to ask what meds they had him on.

"I guess the instructor should be here soon, I'm going to get some tea." He stood up and stretched. "Do you want anything?"

I shook my head. "No. Thanks though." As I watched him walk toward the coffee station, I couldn't help my curiosity. *I wonder how he'll drink without it falling out of the hole...*

People trickled into the room, and conversations echoed off the walls.

"Hey! Jesus loves you!" The preacher's wife waved at me as she entered.

How did she get in here? "Hey, did you just get out?"

"Yep. Got out yesterday. Funny that we'd end up together." She grinned.

"I know, right?" I feigned happiness. *Am I going to have to listen to her for the duration of the hospitalization program? Thankfully the seats next to me are already occupied, so she can't sit there.*

She found a seat a few chairs down. "This is going to be fun! I'm glad that I know someone."

I smiled, but it didn't reach my eyes. *Why does hearing that Jesus loves me irritate me so much? Why isn't it like "bless you" after a sneeze? It irritates me. A lot. It's like Jesus doesn't know I exist. I feel abandoned.*

Since I was a kid, I studied and memorized the bible to find an answer to why I was born this way. Born with a rare disease, my life consisted of hospitalizations, surgeries, and doctor's visits. Once I turned eighteen, every children's program helping with hospital bills dropped me like a hot potato. After all, now I was an adult, and there were no adult programs. I rolled my eyes.

Constant hospitalizations maxed out my health insurance consistently, cost me the jobs I painstakingly found, got me evicted, and even forced me into bankruptcy. My credit got decimated.

My fellow graduates from school and university got beautiful homes and great jobs, but I couldn't. It's hard to watch people you started with succeed and yourself fail epically through no fault of your own.

So no, Jesus didn't love me. Clenching my fists, I drove my nails into my palms.

He never healed me like he allegedly cured all those people in the bible. Unable to have a decent life, I hovered just above the poverty line so that I couldn't get any assistance. He either didn't know I existed, hated me, or he didn't care. I fought back tears

That's how I ended up in the psych ward. I had enough of failing and being behind. I was tired of struggling and being sick. Fed up with never having something nice, having a house too small for my family, and what I saw as - if there was a god - his wrath. So I tried to kill myself.

"I told you that I was sent for you." The preacher's wife leaned over the person next to me.

I cursed mentally. "I guess we'll see, won't we?"

The door to the room opened, and a staff member peeked in, calling my name.

"Yes?"

"Can you come follow me?" He spoke softly, with a gentle smile.

"No. What for?" *I didn't do anything that would warrant a staff member to look for me, and I'm not about to be trapped and sent to the mod again.*

He looked at my instructor.

"It's no big deal. It's only a drug test." She waved it off.

"I'm not taking a drug test. I don't do drugs. Plus, I've been here for a few days now, and nobody else took one." I furrowed my brows.

"Well, you have to take a drug test. It's mandatory." He entered the room fully.

"I will not." I crossed my arms. *Maybe they expect me to scream and make a scene, but I won't give them the satisfaction.*

"If you don't come, we'll have to make you come." His eyes bored into mine.

"You can't touch me. The legal paperwork that was signed before I got here said that you're not allowed to restrain me or grab me in any way." I huffed.

Thank God I chose that. People in such a mental crisis that they need to be admitted shouldn't be presented with legal paperwork to sign. It's a nasty trick, especially because the psych ward puts those who refuse to sign on a seventy-two-hour hold.

The staff member leaned against the door, exchanging looks with the instructor.

"If you test everyone in this room, THEN you can test me. There is no way I, the only black person in the room, will be the only one getting tested for drugs." *I hate to make it about race, but it's obvious that they assumed I was the only junkie in the room.*

He sighed deeply. "Let me see what I can do." He slipped away.

Shifting in her chair, the instructor looked away with raised eyebrows.

The staff member never came back.

• • •

It took a while to adjust to the program. I experienced many mood swings that I couldn't explain rationally. Everything and everyone seemed to become a trigger for me, so I tried to lay low. When the instructor asked me a question, I avoided it and asked if I could leave the room to regroup.

The program lasted longer than predicted. *It's because of that pastor's wife who keeps annoying me.* After I missed leveling up to the next class for the second time, I went to talk to her.

"Hey." I approached her in the cafeteria lunch line. "Can you stop talking to me about Jesus? It's really triggering." *Maybe I can appeal to the minister inside of her.*

She stood firmly. "I can't do that. Jesus told me to tell you."

"Jesus doesn't like me. It would be nice if you respected my request and left me alone." I squared my shoulders.

"You feel like that because you probably have a devil, but I'm going to keep praying for you."

Shaking my head, I laughed. "Just because I don't want to be harassed by you, doesn't mean I have a devil. You should respect my request. If you want to pray, go ahead, but you don't have to tell me about it every moment … unless you're doing it for attention like the Pharisees."

Her brow furrowed. "I'm no Pharisee-"

"Then act like it." I grabbed my drink roughly and walked away before I lost it.

From then on, she sat on the floor in the corner of the classroom with her knees drawn to her chest, glaring at me and ignoring the instructor. Sometimes, she would groan under her breath or sleep on the floor.

Such erratic behavior. I hope she ends up back on the mod.

● ● ●

After two weeks, I finally showed enough mental stability to transfer to the Intensive Outpatient program. *This program is also every day, but at least it's only half a day. No lunch, though. At least if I experience strong emotions in this class, unless I go psycho, I'll be sent back to the Partial Hospitalization Program instead of the mod.*

When I arrived, I saw the girl who parrots.

She smiled when she saw me and beckoned me to sit with her. "I'm so glad to see someone I know."

"Me too." I let out a sigh of relief. "Where is the curly-haired guy?"

"He's been through this whole program before, so he decided to run. I don't think they'll go after him though. It's not like he escaped from the mod. I have to stay because I'm too unstable." She rolled her eyes.

"I guess I'm unstable too then." I chuckled. "We all are here."

She nodded, shifting in her chair.

The new instructor slid into the classroom, her back close to the wall. Her large eyes darted around.

Is she in the wrong room? She looks more like a runway model than a therapist.

After introducing herself, she presented a woman whose hands were balled tightly in a fist with blond hair stuck to her face by tiny dots of perspiration.

The second one is a student from a local university. A future therapist. Did they run to class?

The girl who parrots and I traded looks as the woman with large eyes spoke. In a shaky voice, she explained what we would be doing in class that day.

Ohhhh. They're scared. I laughed.

"To get to know each other, let's take turns introducing ourselves. Tell us your name and something you'd like to share about yourself. It can be your diagnosis ..."

I bet you wanna know that the most. I held back a smile.

"... what you do for fun, coping skills you use, where you work ... stuff like that." She wrung her hands.

They started on the other side of the room. From a truck driver driving across the country to a transgendered person having relationship problems, there were people from all walks of life.

A slightly chubby and cute lady cleared her throat. She pushed her blonde hair aside with manicured nails. "I'm an ER nurse. I've been having trouble at work due to being admitted to the psych ward. My superiors feel I can't be trusted with patients, so they've been trying to keep me from coming back."

So stupid. She worked in the ER and saw things most of us will never see. It makes sense that some of it would get to her. You'd think that those in the health field would know better when it comes to mental health issues because everyone needs a doctor every once in a while, even doctors.

While she talked about what put her in the ward, I zoned out, as usual. Suddenly, the girl who parroted stood on her chair, pointing at the nurse while screaming.

"You! You killed him!" She growled through gritted teeth, and her mascara caused black tears to run down her face. "You did this to my baby!" Jumping off of her chair, she threw it towards the nurse.

The two instructors bolted out of the room. Over the loudspeaker, a woman's voice called a code and color to request the assistance of all nearby staff.

"I'm gonna kill you!" The girl who parrots shrieked, pointing at the nurse again.

We all sat there in the room, numb due to the many times we saw things like this happen on the mod.

She ran to attack the nurse, who now stood, prepared to protect herself. A whole team of security busted through the door. They grabbed her and dragged her out of the room kicking, screaming, and threatening the other patient.

It's entirely possible to hurt someone in here without any interference from the rest of us. The medication makes us lethargic. Nobody is strong enough to fight against this medicine, nor does anyone care enough to. I glanced over at the nurse to see if she was rattled. *I don't know why I'm looking, it's not like I plan to help...*

"Okay." The instructor bit her lip. "Maybe we should do something else instead of finishing this exercise." She looked over at her assistant.

The assistant nodded her head, her blond ponytail bouncing fervently.

"Let's talk about how SSRIs work..."

The silence was deafening. We all just sat there waiting to be instructed.

"Okay..." She turned sideways as she wrote on the board, keeping her eyes on the rest of the class.

Since it was someone I knew, what happened before bothered

me. I asked around to find out what I missed. *It turns out the nurse was talking about one of her infant patients who passed away, which triggered the girl who parrots. I had no idea she suffered from PTSD. No wonder since her toddler died in her arms. It's even sadder since she almost finished all the steps to get out of the psych ward. Now she's back to square one. That won't happen to me. I'm getting out of here, once and for all.*

• • •

"Happy New Year's Eve!" The instructor smiled widely.

Seriously, we even have to come here for New Year's Eve.

Everyone chorused a well-trained response. Someone brought cookies to class to share. As the plastic container passed around the class, I chose putty from the basket in the middle of the classroom. It was filled with different toys and stress relievers to play with during class without disrupting the lesson. There were stress balls, fidget spinners, slime, putty, and little puzzle games.

I've been feeling anxious all day without knowing why, so the putty will keep me present and give me something else to think about.

"We're going to split into two teams and play a game today. This side of the room…" She motioned to her left. "Against that side of the room." She motioned to her right. "The first team to get to eight wins the game!" She flashed a smile.

My heart dropped.

As everyone moved their chairs to their respective side of the room, she laid out the rules. "I'm going to give each person standing at the board a word or phrase from one of these cards." She held up a stack of yellow cards. "The person at the board will draw a clue while the rest of you try to guess and spell what's on the card. We will go back and forth." After passing a card to a short trans guy standing at the board, she prepared the timer.

I raised my hand. "Can I sit this one out?"

"Well, it's no fun unless everyone plays." She pouted.

Blegh. "I don't like competitive games. Can I just watch?"

She looked around. "Does anyone else feel the same way?"

Of course, no one agrees. I groaned. My heart thumped in my throat, and I began to sweat.

Suddenly, she changed her mind. "Okay, you can pass out the clues."

This lady is more observant than I gave her credit for. Whew! I can easily strike up a conversation with a stranger, but competitive games freak me out.

The game finally ended. *Somehow I made it through, now if only my brain would shut up.* My mind kept replaying the conversation with the teacher before the game started. Feelings of embarrassment flooded my body, and I hyperventilated. I rushed out of the class and found refuge in the lobby, collecting myself.

I don't want to go back to class. Can't I stay on the couch here? My head throbbed terribly. From the lobby, I could hear the instructor moving into the lesson connected to the game. I stretched out on the couch, closing my eyes. My mind raced. Scanning my thoughts, I looked for a good memory to focus on.

My grandma's laugh is a good memory… But she's dead now.

I imagined myself singing in concert, a dream I used to have long ago. It made me think of my dad.

He had such a wonderful voice… But he's dead.

I squeezed my eyes tightly, trying to think about good times.

It was fun to hang out with my cousin and party. Cool things used to happen when we got together…But we don't party anymore.

"Okay, I've had enough of this." I sighed, slowly sitting upright. Noticing the putty still in my hands, I stretched and played around with it until I felt calm. Calming down took longer than anticipated due to an unexpected interruption.

Another patient with mousy blond hair in two braids came to check on me.

"I'm okay." I beat her to the punch.

"Are you coming back in? Do you need me to sit out here with you?" She wrung her hands.

I stood up. "I think I can go back in now." I walked towards the classroom.

Here's hoping that I don't have another panic attack any time soon.

• • •

After a few days, things fell into a rhythm. Nobody had any outbursts, or issues that were disruptive, except one guy who had a seizure during class. *I think he had a seizure disorder to begin with. We all seem to be becoming more stable. I'm able to use the coping skills I learned and haven't had any panic attacks. The desire to end it all is always in the back of my mind, but I feel my mood is more stable.*

I must be feeling good because they've finally got my medications right, and the preacher's wife no longer comes to class. Who knows what happened to her, and who cares?

About seven days into the New Year, I completed the class and graduated from the hospital. Until the teacher talked to me about graduation, I never knew it was possible. *Who graduates from a psych ward? That would make me certified crazy.*

On graduation day, all the remaining students brought the graduates little gifts, cookies, and cakes to celebrate.

It wasn't a huge graduation, and none of my family could attend. I received a diploma-like certificate with the psych ward's name and the therapist's signature on it, along with a keychain. Also, the whole class sat in a circle while everyone said nice things about me.

Once I completed all things related to my mental health and entered back into normal life, I struggled to adjust.

I would wake up on the weekends in a panic, thinking I'd missed the Partial Hospitalization program even though it finished. During the day, I would mostly stay in the house because I was used to only being able to go out for a short time. Whenever I encountered people getting overly excited, I kept thinking they needed to stop or the staff would throw them in the closet.

The fact that I wasn't getting any work made it harder for things to go back to normal.

This sucks. I'm not getting hired. The medication I'm on made me gain forty pounds over three months. I knew when I started working as an independent contractor that the acting field relies heavily on looks and personality. Getting hired depends less on my experience and more on my ability to get along with others.

I tried being my authentic self, but my real self isn't the most fun person to be around. I have no choice but to put the mask from before the psych ward back on.

On top of being unable to find work, my disease also flared up. Hemorrhaging and blood clots kept sending me to the hospital, getting one procedure after another, and I laid around at home recovering instead of working.

I had hoped that I'd be in a better place financially this year. Things have to get better soon.

4

MY DOT

I feel so lonely. Having a long-term illness weighed on me and the people around me. My son, daughter, and Pocket spent a lot of time taking care of me and hanging out in my hospital room. But my friends all disappeared over time. People don't have the stamina to have a sick friend, and the sick friend doesn't have the stamina to reach out or stay in contact.

One day, Pocket and I suddenly realized we no longer had any friends. We looked at each other in confusion.

"We used to have friends, didn't we?" *I don't remember the last time we went out with friends - or even my cousin, with whom I've always been close.* "Where did they go?"

"I don't know, babe." He didn't look up from the screen of his phone but continued to play his game. "I guess we gotta get some more."

With my health, how would that even work? "How are we

going to do that? Where are we going to find them? The bar?" I brainstormed ideas. "We used to have fun at the bar…"

"I don't know babes, but right now you just need to focus on getting better." He still didn't look up.

I don't want to focus on my health. For years I've done nothing but, and it didn't get me anywhere. Nodding, I went to get the dog's leash. The sunshine came through whatever crack it could find.

It feels like I need proper motivation to get better, but my options are limited. I can only do something that doesn't take a lot of physical exertion, doesn't cost a lot of money, and can be done from a hospital bed if necessary. Befriending someone should work.

• • •

I wiped my face as the heat caused beads of sweat to roll like sideburns down my face. My dog panted at the end of her leash as we walked back to our house. In the distance, I saw two girls standing in my driveway. They waved at us happily as we approached. At about twenty feet away, I spotted little black name tags on the left side of their dresses.

"Hi!" They smiled.

"Church of Jesus Christ of Latter-Day Saints?" I doubled over with my hands on my knees, catching my breath. *Man, it's hot out.*

"Yes!" They chorused. Both girls had thick blond hair and glasses, wearing modern prairie dresses. Beautiful and very young, they were about 19 or 20 years old.

"We are sister missionaries for the Church of Jesus Christ of

Latter-Day Saints, and we wanted to know if you have some time to have a lesson with us. One smiled, and the other squinted in the sun with her hands clasped.

Not Jesus again.

"Not really." I shook my head, adjusting the leash in my hand. *Even if I do have plenty of time, there's no need for you to know because I don't plan on giving it to you.*

"That's okay. We can always come back another time if you'd like?"

Ugh! I don't want to be mean... "Like when?" I watched as my dog investigated their dresses.

"Whenever you're free!"

"Well..." I hesitated. "Not sure when I'd be available. I have a lot of health issues and spend a lot of time in the hospital."

"Oh no!" Both of them clutched their chests in synchronization, gasping. "So sorry to hear that."

I pulled my dog away from them. "Yeah, so it'll be hard to set a date."

"Okay, well we'll just keep stopping by occasionally to check on you, how's that?"

That sounds harmless. "Alright. That would be nice." I inched up my driveway.

"We'll see you later!" They smiled cheerfully and handed me a card with what seemed like their contact information and a rendition of Jesus on the back of it.

I walked as quickly as possible up my driveway and onto my front step, turning to see how far away they had gotten in that amount of time. I couldn't see them anymore.

Great, now I've got some missionaries to hound me about Jesus.

• • •

The sister missionaries had been chasing me for about a year, leaving cards and sticky notes with scriptures on the door, and stopping by periodically to check on me. They usually met my son, who was around their age, and he would forward messages from them. They even checked up on my family while I was in the psych ward.

Even though I'd rush into the house without letting them get a word in or not open the door when they rang, they never gave up.

From the time I met the missionaries a year ago to the day I ran into them in my driveway; I battled complications from my syndrome. If not at the hospital, I was home in bed. The more I struggled with my physical health, the more I struggled with my mental health. I fell into a depression; I rarely would get out of bed, even when I could. *Even if things are bad, I'm not returning to the psych ward, no matter who suggests it.*

Dragging myself out of bed, I forced myself to get ready and eat something.

"Mom." My son came through the garage entrance. "I ran into some Elders."

Elders? "Who are they?" I wrinkled my nose as I walked down the stairs.

Shrugging, he locked the door behind him. "Some type of guy missionaries from that Church. At any rate, I told them that I was very busy and couldn't talk. It's not a lie."

I nodded. *He's busy and so am I.* "I saw some missionaries not long ago, but they were girls. I told them I was always either busy or sick, so I didn't have the time. How come they always seem to stop us and never Pocket?"

"Right? The Elders follow me everywhere. I see them at work, at the grocery store, and they're always waiting for me in the driveway when I come home." He made his way into the kitchen.

I watched him make a sandwich. *I've got to figure out a nice way to get these missionaries to stop coming to our house for good.*

The front door squeaked, announcing that Pocket had come home from work.

He brought me a beautiful bouquet! "Hey, babes!" I smiled as he made his way down the hallway.

"Do you have something to tell me?" He held out the flowers.

I raised my eyebrows. "About what?"

"About these flowers. They were outside, leaning against the door when I came home."

Is he angry? "No? I don't know anything about them."

"Well, they must be for you because nobody else in this house would receive flowers." He headed to the kitchen and grabbed a vase.

Okay. He's not angry. "Did they have a card or a note?" I followed him, racking my brain. "Who would bring me flowers?"

"Nope, someone just left them. Makes me wonder what you're up to while I'm at work." He grinned and kissed me on the forehead.

"Maybe the missionaries? That's the only thing I can think

of. They know I've been sick, but they'd normally leave a note. I don't know."

"I don't know either." He shrugged.

"Well… they're young. They probably didn't realize that flowers mysteriously appearing without a note could ruin a relationship." I laughed, rubbing the back of my neck. *Thankfully he's not the jealous type.*

"Next time you see those missionaries, tell them you almost lost your relationship because of them." He chuckled.

However, I never spoke to the missionaries because whenever I saw them walking the neighborhood, I would run into my house and act like I wasn't there if they knocked.

● ● ●

The sky slowly darkened as I walked along the street. My dog pulled me toward her usual field to run and go to the bathroom. Summer passed quickly, and it was getting near fall, so it got dark earlier in the day. I spotted two Elders across the road with white shirts sporting that infamous name tag and dress pants, straddling their bikes.

"Hey!" They called my name, waving as I approached the field.

How do they know my name? Great, I can't avoid them. "Hi." *I don't even know if they heard me.*

"We went to see your son, but he was busy. He's a really busy guy."

Are they clueless or pretending to be? "Yeah, I've been keeping him busy with all my health problems." I let my dog off the leash. She ran into the field. "This is one of the few times I've been able to walk the dog."

"Sorry to hear that." They spoke to me from across the street. *I'm so glad they stayed over there.*

"We can come and do a lesson with you, even if you don't feel well. You could just sit on the couch with your son and listen. You don't have to do much." They smiled charmingly.

I can't lie. My stomach twisted in knots. *These kids are so nice, respectful, and YOUNG ... Why are they so young?*

"I'll think about it." My dog ran back to me, and I attached her leash.

"That's all we ask."

As I turned to head home, I glanced back. "Be careful out there on those bikes. It's getting dark, and the coyotes are out."

"Okay!" Their eyes darted around as if one was about to run up to them at that very moment.

On my way back to the house, I debated letting those Elders in. *Maybe one day.*

• • •

In the beginning of December, the Elders and missionaries had been taking turns trying to get us to schedule a lesson with them for over a year, eighteen months if I count the time spent in the psych ward, without success.

"Let me braid your hair." *I think I'm feeling well enough now after two weeks. I've missed spending time with Theo like this.* Focusing on my son's hair as he sat between my knees on the living room floor, I braided the long and curly strands.

Suddenly, the doorbell rang, interrupting our conversation. We locked eyes, engaging in a telepathic debate to convince each other to answer the door. He lost and jumped up.

I couldn't hear the conversation between him and the missionaries, but I heard giggling. It sounded like they were familiar with him.

"Mom, the missionaries are here!" His voice echoed down the hall. "They want to know if they can give a lesson."

I sighed, rubbing my head. *Looks like that persistent bear I've been running from finally caught up with me. It's been more than a year at this point.* "Well, tell them to come back in a couple of hours when I'm done with your hair. They earned it."

A few hours later, my son opened the door for the sister missionaries, escorting them in before disappearing.

Two young girls smiled as I invited them to sit on the couch with me. They introduced themselves as Sister Bullard and Sister Robison. As soon as they sat on the couch, I spilled my guts.

"Sorry that it took so long for me to invite you in. It's just that I've been through a lot this past year. I've been to the psych ward, hospitalized multiple times, and-"

They glanced at each other with one eyebrow raised. It stopped me in my tracks.

"Oh, we aren't the same missionaries as before." Sister Robison, a beautiful brunette with green eyes hidden behind a pair of glasses, tucked her hair behind her ear. "I arrived this week."

Sister Bullard, with dark sun-kissed hair and a slight tan, hesitated. "...And I've only got a few weeks left."

"Oh." My brain quickly recalculated. I filled them in on everything that happened since the other missionaries tried to meet with me. As I spoke I began to cry, a wave of relief washing over me. *That was what I needed. No advice or judgment. I just needed someone to listen.*

"We want to let you know that Heavenly Father sent us here to you." Sister Robison looked deeply into my eyes.

That's probably stuff they say to get inside people's houses. I leaned back and crossed my arms. "Prove it."

"Every morning before we go out, we pray to find out who Heavenly Father wants us to see that day." Sister Robison pulled out a cell phone. A map appeared on the screen that had five dots on it. "After we prayed, Heavenly Father gave us five people to go to, and yours was one of them." She showed me the dot that represented me.

Sister Bullard nodded.

"That's my dot?" I sniffled.

A big smile graced her face. "Yep."

I paused, sitting in silence for a few minutes.

If that's my dot, maybe God does care that I exist… Maybe he'll help me get out of this vicious cycle. And if he knows I exist, and he cares, he'll give me friends too.

"Pocket, my partner, and I noticed that we lost our friends over time, and now there's no one left. I really want to have friends again. Someone with whom I can be myself, laugh at silly things, and do new things. I don't want to be alone."

"We'll be your friends!"

I want to believe them so badly. "Really?"

"Yeah, we'll be your friends. We can come over, hang out, and teach you a lesson too!" Sister Robison clapped cheerfully.

I bit my lip, debating. *They're young enough to be my son's friends. Whatever, what have I got to lose?* "Okay! You'll be my friends!"

The front door opened, and I caught a glimpse of Pocket as he walked into the kitchen. He just got home from work.

"Hey, babes, the missionaries are here." My tone was happy, but it also hid a warning. *I don't want him to complain about the Elders if he saw them outside while the sisters were there.*

He peeked over the countertop, nodded his head, and then headed upstairs to our room.

I turned back to the missionaries. "Are you sure God said that was my dot?"

"Absolutely." The blond nodded.

"Okay..." I clasped my hands together. *This better not be a lie.*

They spent about an hour teaching me from a book called 'Preach My Gospel' and going through the scriptures with me. I knew most of it already from my extensive study of the Bible.

Before leaving, they handed me a blue book with a thin cover. "Read all of the introduction pages as well as chapter one in the book of Nephi."

"Alright." I examined the cover of the books they left, cozying up with it on the couch. *Maybe there's something I missed that will finally change things.*

5

THE BOOK AND THE CHURCH

"The Book of Mormon, Another Testament of Jesus Christ." I ran my fingers across the lettering on the cover. Sinking deeply into the couch, I read the introduction. "The book was written by a whole bunch of prophets who wrote everything down on gold plates…"

Gold plates? That's an expensive revelation.

"Abridged by a guy named Mormon, hence the name, and delivered to his son Moroni who added some stuff, and then passed on to Joseph Smith who supposedly translated it by the gift and power of God."

Sounds fantastical…

I turned to the next page titled 'The Testimony of Three Witnesses'. "The witnesses: Oliver Cowdery, David Whitmer, and Martin Harris all testified that the book was true and they saw the golden plates with their own eyes."

Never heard of these guys in history, but okay. Let's see where this goes.

The following part consisted of 'The Testimony of Eight Witnesses', more people who claimed to have seen the plates. However, they got to touch them. I read over the list of names.

They were all related. Maybe they worked together as a family and made up the fact that they saw the plates - or even that they exist!

I moved on to the next section, 'The Testimony Of The Prophet Joseph Smith.' "Joseph claimed an angel called Moroni visited and told him about the golden plates as well as two stones used to translate them. Moroni came back two other times to relay more information."

This is crazy...

I whipped out my cell phone, scrolling through my contacts until I found the number the missionaries gave me before they left. My fingers flew across the screen as I composed my message.

"Hey, I started reading the book you gave me, and I have a few questions. What is the Joseph Smith-History in the Pearl of Great Price? Will I find that in the Book of Mormon? Some of the Three and Eight Witnesses have the same last names. Are they related to each other? (Like family members?) Are these plates magical? And is it true the plates were in Manchester, NY? Sorry for all the questions."

After a few moments, they texted an even longer paragraph back.

I almost don't want to read it, but I'd better.

"The Joseph Smith-History is the story of how Joseph saw God and Jesus Christ and was inspired to find and translate the gold plates into what is now The Book of Mormon. The Pearl of Great Price is a separate book of scripture. If you want, we could get one for you. Some witnesses have the same last names because they were related (Whitmers and Smiths)..."

I knew it! This is probably a scam.

"The plates were what the ancient inhabitants of the Americas wrote on to keep their records, kind of like journals. They were passed down through generations and then hidden on a hill in NY by the prophet Moroni. Moroni is the angel who showed Joseph Smith where the plates were. It's hard to explain through text, so if it still doesn't make sense let us know."

Although I was skeptical, I kept going. I almost finished what the missionaries asked me to read so I figured that reading the first chapter of Nephi wouldn't take that long. I was wrong. I instantly got sucked into the storyline and couldn't come up for air if I tried.

This book reads like a movie script.

The main character's name was Nephi. His father was some lower-level prophet, not huge like Moses or anyone from the Bible, but a prophet nonetheless.

"Although they lived in Jerusalem, they made plans to leave because the Lord showed Nephi's dad that Jerusalem would suffer destruction. But first, Nephi and his brothers had to get their property and valuables back from his uncle Laban, who had stolen them. They eventually got everything back except for the law of Moses, which was engraved on brass. Laban refused to return it. So they waited until Laban was drunk, lying in the street asleep, and decapitated him. That's how they got the brass back.

If he was drunk and laid out on the street, did they really have to kill him? Okay ... I guess this is all backstory?

It was late. *Would the missionaries even be awake at this hour?*

I fired off a text message anyway.

"I know I said I'd wait till you return, but I just got to the part in Nephi where the main guy kills Laban (because Laban took their property and valuables and refused to return the plates). He took Laban's servant, Zoram, and they made an oath with each other. Did all this happen before they came to the Americas? Is this like backstory?"

My phone dinged, telling me they were awake later than they should be.

"Yes, most of the first book of Nephi takes place while they're still in Jerusalem. It's background as to how they came to America, and we can totally explain when we come."

I kept reading until late into the night, glued to the living room couch. The sound of a door closing caught my attention. Pocket entered the house after his last nightly cigarette break.

"This reads like a movie!" I bounced with excitement, hands waving. "And there is so much in here that applies to where we are today politically and as a nation."

As I read parts of the book out loud to him, our son came downstairs to listen. When I finished the chapter, I looked at them with expectation. "Well? What do you think?"

Theo nodded in approval.

Pocket contemplated it for a second. "I've never seen you so excited about a book."

"That's because it reads like a script. You can literally see the events in the book playing out like a film in your mind." I looked into his eyes. *Please see what I see.*

"That's crazy." My son raised his eyebrows.

Pocket shrugged, parroting what he said before. "Yeah, I've just never seen you so excited about a book before."

Theo always says 'that's crazy' when he hears about something cool or amazing. They're not going to match my enthusiasm, but at least they seem intrigued. That's good enough for now.

Nodding to myself, I put my feet on the couch and dove back into the book. *I'm definitely not going to sleep tonight.*

● ○ ●

Pulling the cover over my head, I tried to block the afternoon sunlight beaming through the blinds. I knew it before I was even fully awake, I was depressed. *I slept the morning away without meaning to. I'd done so well since I got out of the psych ward and started taking the proper combination of medications, but today my body feels like a weight is crushing it, and I feel trapped in a tunnel unable to escape.* I tossed the cover off my head and kicked my legs over the bed.

I might as well get up. Can't be in bed all day.

Making my way to the bathroom, I grabbed my toothbrush.

Should I shower first? I looked in the direction of the shower. The yellow and white shower curtain brightened the room. *Nah, I don't feel like the hassle.*

As I stared at myself in the mirror while brushing my teeth, I sighed. *My reflection doesn't look like how I think I look at all. They say that's what happens as you age; one day you look young and vibrant in the mirror, and the next thing you know, you look like a complete stranger.*

I look like an old stranger. It's going to be a bad day…

Fighting the urge to crawl back into bed, I opened my dresser drawer to grab my meds. As I searched my room for a water bottle, I found the blue book given to me by the missionaries hidden under a pile of things. *How did it get there? I remember bringing it upstairs, but the rest is a blur.*

Once I located my water bottle, I took my medication.

I don't really feel like reading more of the book. Despite my hesitation, something deep inside me pushed me to continue. Obediently, I opened the book and searched for where I left off. *I was somewhere around 1 Nephi 17.*

"Nephi and his family traveled through the wilderness. It was hard on them. The women even traveled while pregnant, and they gave birth outdoors. How uncomfortable. They ate raw meat to survive."

Ew! Disgusting!

They traveled in the wilderness for about eight years looking for a place to live near the water, until they could cross the ocean to travel to the Americas, their promised land.

Hmmm. Kinda like the Israelites in the Bible…

"After they set up camp near the sea, the Lord asked Nephi to build a ship. He showed Nephi where to get all of the supplies…"

This is boring. I'm going to take a break.

Surfing social media, I sighed. *My mind just isn't in it.*

The heaviness in my body made it hard to even turn the pages. *Maybe if I sit on the couch again, I'll feel better.*

I crept down the stairs and entered the hall. The house was quiet, no one was home. *It's the perfect time to focus on the book.*

I picked up where I left off, as I sunk into the couch. Before I knew it I reached the beginning of 2 Nephi. All was going well until I ran into a set of scriptures that stopped me dead in my tracks.

"And he had caused the cursing to come upon them, yea, even a sore cursing, because of their iniquity. For behold, they had hardened their hearts against him, that they had become like flint; wherefore, as they were white, and exceedingly fair and delightsome, that they might not be enticing to my people the Lord God did cause a skin of blackness to come upon them.

And thus saith the Lord God: I will cause that they shall be loathsome unto thy people, save they shall repent of their iniquities.

And cursed shall be the seed of him that mixeth with their seed; for they shall be cursed even with the same cursing. And the Lord spake it, and it was done."

And so am I. This is blatant racism!

The scripture went on to talk about the black Lamanites who, according to the story, were lazy, idle, and full of mischief and cunning.

If this is how this church feels about black people, I think I'm done with this book.

I slammed the book onto the couch.

It was bad enough that I was depressed, now I'm depressed AND angry. Pulling my phone out of my pocket, my fingers typed fast.

"So ... I've read through until 2 Nephi 5. But when I got to 5:22-5:25 I instantly wanted to stop reading. I'm not sure why this book makes such a big deal about the white ones having God's favor and black people being lazy, mischievous, sneaky, and cursed. Given today's racial climate, it pulled me straight out of the story. The first couple of times, I could ignore it because it made no comparison to any other race. This part broke my heart. I don't wanna read anymore."

After adding a few crying emojis, I pressed send and took a few deep breaths to calm my nerves.

I want to scream! Or complain to my son or Pocket, but I'm alone. Why would the missionaries hand out a book that discriminates against black people to actual black people? It makes more sense to leave us alone if you know all of this horrible information about us is in the book.

Suddenly, my phone dinged.

"We're so sorry that part upset you. We can totally see where you're coming from. However, there's an explanation that's hard to give over text. Know that God loves ALL of his children, regardless of skin color. In 2 Nephi 26:33, it tells us that God loves everyone, whether black or white. Sister Robison's little brother is black and she had the same question about that scripture. It's more comparing their hearts rather than the color of their skin..."

But it IS about skin. It literally says so. I continued to read the message.

"...They all looked the same and the Lamanites turned

wicked so God made them have dark skin so the Nephites would know who they were. He could have done any number of things to tell the two nations apart, he just changed their skin color. It has nothing to do with the marking of the curse. You'll see as you keep reading that the people with black skin become highly favored by the Lord and the white-skinned people turn wicked and are destroyed. We know that part without context can sound bad, but please continue to trust us and meet with us tomorrow. Remember how you felt that night we met, and don't forget that God chose your dot!"

My anger subsided as the excitement, relief, and awe I felt then came flooding back.

They prayed to see who to meet, and I was hand-selected by God as one of the five people. I mean, the black people DO win at the end... maybe it's not so bad?

After giving it some thought, I responded.

"Ok. I'm sad, but I feel like you chose my dot for a reason. We'll still meet tomorrow. I really hope God likes me."

They answered quickly.

"We promise you that he loves you! Pray on your knees that you'll have peace until we talk tomorrow. Is it possible for us to come at 1 instead?"

After agreeing, I stared at the heart emoji they had sent hoping that I could get past what I read and make it to the end. I paused.

Wait a minute. Every sister missionary and Elder that came to our door, or stopped us in the street, was white. Perhaps the whole church is white. If it is, will there even be a place for me and my family? Pocket and Jo are white, but Theo and I aren't. Our family is interracial.

How would my son and I fit in a place made for white people - if it's true that it's a white church? Would they understand the dynamics of our blended family? Pocket and I didn't differentiate between our children. Whether or not related by blood, they're just our kids, so Jo is my daughter, and Theo is his son.

Part of me wanted to stop reading because of the strong emotions bubbling up. Some of those emotions were good, others not so much. I decided to think about it for a bit. *After all, it will do me no good to make a rash decision about the church without giving it a chance.*

• • •

The missionaries came prepared for our next lesson. They brought an older member of the church with them. I offered our blue lounge chair to the tall gentleman with a shaved bald head and glasses.

Of course, they'd bring a black man. I laughed to myself.

He introduced himself as Matthew White. His gentle, fatherly disposition instantly made me feel less combative and more willing to hear what he had to say as he slid smoothly past the small talk into a conversation of more substance. It was as if the missionaries weren't even there.

"How long have you been in the church?" I leaned forward in my seat.

He looked up as if trying to remember. "I married my wife in the seventies, and after that, I was in the military… I joined in the South in the eighties with two other black guys. We were the only black guys there." He smiled softly.

Geez! Being the only black guys must have been rough back then. But it couldn't have been that bad... He's been a member for forty years!

"If you were the only black guys, why did you join? I furrowed my brows.

"I was a member of a different church, and most of my family members went there as well - they believed the same thing I did at the time. But when I heard about the doctrine of the LDS church, I agreed with it more. So I joined." He chuckled. "My family wasn't happy when I changed churches, but I didn't care. I had to do what was best for me."

I don't know about this... I've always heard that the Latter-Day Saints were a cult.

"I heard that the church worships Joseph Smith."

He shook his head. "Nah, he's just the guy who started the church. We don't worship him; we acknowledge that he was the prophet who founded the church." He sat up in his chair, looking into my eyes. "The church is a good place to be. They've got good messages, not a preacher yelling at you over a pulpit. And the people are really nice. Come and see. You'll like it."

I tried to soak in everything he told me. *The whole 'dark skin being a curse' thing still bothers me, though.*

When I asked him about it, he waved his hand as if swatting a fly. "You don't have to believe in everything right now. Take it a little at a time."

Thanking the missionaries and Matthew for coming, I stood

at the entrance to see them off. Pocket sat outside on the front step of our house and lit up a cigarette. Despite being a non-smoker, occasionally I'd sit with him while he did. Today was one of those days.

He looked at me while a breeze made the smoke blow in the opposite direction. "Careful of that man, he's got a gift."

"How do you know?" I stared into his eyes, intrigued.

Blowing out smoke as he spoke, he rubbed his chin. "He asked me about the game that was on earlier. When I looked up, I saw him, and I knew."

Surprised, I blurted out everything Matthew and I discussed and then waited for his response.

He nodded as if taking it all in, but he didn't say anything.

Pocket rarely says anything about religious things because he lacks experience with church or reading the Bible. Even though he didn't say much, I can tell that Matthew White piqued his interest in the church.

• • •

A couple of weeks later, Pocket, Theo, and I stood awkwardly in the empty church vestibule, waiting for the missionaries. It was our first time at the church, and the missionaries wanted to show us the Christmas festivities organized that night. We exchanged looks. *Where are the missionaries and when will they come?*

Suddenly, a door opened in front of us, and a person came out. We perked up. *Maybe they came to greet us.* They walked past us. I sent a text message to the missionaries.

"We're inside. Maybe we're at the wrong church…"

I stared at my phone, awaiting a response, but it remained silent. "They aren't answering. Maybe we're at the wrong church."

At that moment, a man walking down the hall appeared to be approaching. He saw us but continued on his way without saying or doing anything.

"You'd think these people would notice how awkward we are and point us in the right direction." I frowned, opening and closing my hands.

My family shrugged. We stood around a bit longer.

"We should go." I looked at the guys for confirmation.

Theo glanced around. "If you want to, we can go."

"It's just… Can't these people tell that we're new and don't know where to go or what to do?" I rubbed my temple. "Can't they tell how awkward we are? All people who don't belong somewhere look awkward. Where are the greeters? Why do missionaries invite people if there are no members to show them where to go? They could at least put out a sign to point us in the right direction." I pursed my lips, frowning at my phone. "Yeah… let's go."

As we got ready to leave, I heard my name. The two missionaries who came to our house scurried down the hall, holding their modern prairie dresses to not trip. "We're sorry, we were waiting for you guys on the other side!"

There's another side? While waiting, I got myself worked up, contrasting their excitement.

"Oh." I said through clenched jaws. *I can't lie in church and say 'it's okay', because it's really not. Thankfully, they don't seem to notice how annoyed I am.*

They walked towards the door that we saw a person come out of earlier. "Everybody is going to want to meet you!" They swung the door open, revealing a gym filled with food, tables, and people.

Instantly, we entered the crowd swarming near the door where the desserts and the line for the meals were.

The missionaries introduced us to random people in line. As everyone wanted to shake our hands, I felt my heart pounding in my throat. I could barely swallow. I tried to keep up with the missionaries.

Someone put their hand out to me to shake. I balled my fist, palms sweaty with anxiety. "I'd rather fist bump". I held my fist out, smiling tightly.

Suddenly, about four fists stuck out, and several people introduced themselves. Overwhelmed, I couldn't hear them. I watched their lips move and bumped my fist against theirs.

Where are Pocket and Theo? I couldn't feel them behind me. Keeping my eyes on the missionaries, I followed them as they made a beeline to a table with enough seats for all of us.

There was a friendly-looking older couple already seated at the table. The missionaries presented us and then disappeared to get food. The couple smiled, introducing themselves as Tim and Kandi Guffey.

Wearing another tight smile, I dropped into a chair on the opposite side of the table. As we made small talk, I found out that Tim used to be a bishop in the church. I stored the information for later. *It'll be good to know a bishop if I run into more problems in the Book of Mormon.*

I surveyed the room. Debating whether we should get up and grab food or hang out at the table with the couple, I glanced at Theo. He seemed to be more at ease, so I decided to follow his lead.

Although we sat only minutes ago, I looked at my son, eyebrows raised. "Should we get food?" My hands shook, my palms were sweaty, and my heart pounded in my throat. I recognized the onset of a panic attack.

"Yeah." He stood.

Pocket and I followed him to the food line, where more people wanted to talk to us.

Despite giving closed-ended answers to people's questions and short version stories of how we met the missionaries, it became more difficult to breathe with each conversation. I rushed through the food line and speed-walked back to my table. *I need to sit before I faint or something. Usually, conversations with strangers come easily to me, but not in a crowd this size. If I were on stage, it would be a different story, but being surrounded by an ocean of people feels like I'm drowning in strangers. It's too much. I don't think I can make it.*

I kept my eyes on my family members and spoke to them as I struggled to control my anxiety. *Just focus on your family. Nobody else is here, there's only you and them.*

Instead of focusing, I gazed around the room. *Everybody in here is white!*

I spotted a light brown family, but I couldn't tell if they were tanned white people or people of color.

Well, at least they're here. I exhaled slowly, poking my food with my fork.

I managed to hold a conversation with Tim and Kandi without panicking. The more we talked, the more it seemed like we were the only people in the room. My anxiety slowly subsided, leaving me in a much better mood. So much that I jumped up to go to the dessert table once I finished my meal.

Circling the table indecisively, I picked up a dessert plate.

"Have you had a brownie yet?" A mousey blond kid asked, waving a brownie.

He looks like he's about six years old. I smiled. "No, are they good?"

Biting into the brownie, he hummed. "You've GOT to try the brownies!" Pointing his finger a hair close to the top of a brownie, he nodded. "These ones right here. You've got to have them!"

"Okay. If you say so…" I picked up the brownie the kid pointed to. Examining it closely, I made sure there was nothing that I didn't like or was allergic to. *It looks fine.* I wanted to thank the kid, but when I looked up, he had disappeared. A quick scan of the room proved fruitless. *Nope. Gone.*

I bit into the brownie. Incredibly moist, the rich and chocolaty taste enveloped my tongue. I cursed mentally. *This brownie is everything!*

Quickly returning to my seat, I spread the gospel of the brownie. Pocket and Theo jumped up to try one. The consensus was that these brownies were the best we ever had.

We seriously need to consider coming back to this church.

● ● ●

One day later, we went back.

"Hey, we have seats saved, so let us know when you're here!" The missionaries texted me as we pulled into the church parking lot.

"Just pulled up." *Talk about timing.*

We strode across the parking lot, dressed in our nicest shirts and jeans. Two Elders wearing white shirts, ties, and huge smiles greeted us at the door. They didn't look like the Elders we met in the past. As they held the door open for us, we spotted the two sister missionaries. They waved and hurried to hug us.

"Follow us. We have a spot picked out!" Sister Bullard smiled, her eyes sparkling.

We followed them to a bench in the middle of the central section of the sanctuary. As soon as we sat down, different members came to greet us and introduce themselves.

Tim and Kandi, from the Christmas festivities the night before, came to shake hands and give me a fist bump. I smiled. *Even though I'm happy to see them, I'm worried. Who will come over next?* My chest tightened. They talked and smiled, but I couldn't focus on what they were saying - or what I was saying. In a daze, I kept glancing at the clock. Thankfully, the conversation ended as quickly as it started, and the couple went back to their seats.

The service was quiet and reverent. A man stood at the pulpit announcing different events the church was having. Slipping into autopilot, it startled me when he asked the congregation to vote for who would be getting an assignment to lead one of the church's programs.

"Are they about to vote?" I looked at Sister Robison, clasping my hands and biting my lip. "We're not registered to vote…"

Giggling, she leaned towards me. "You don't have to register to vote. You can raise your hand if you want, but you don't have to."

I transmitted the message to my family.

We raised our hands to vote when everyone else did.

Moments later, there was a prayer. A group of young pre-teen boys dressed in white shirts, ties, and slacks, got up to make their way to the front of the church. Grabbing trays, they began to walk the aisles, handing a tray to each row. People grabbed something fluffy off the tray and popped it into their mouths.

"This is called sacrament." Sister Robison passed the tray to me, her whisper a stark contrast to the silence in the sanctuary. "Just grab a piece of bread and eat it."

Torn pieces of white, soft, and fluffy sandwich bread slices decorated the pristine silver tray. *This bread has leaven in it. Didn't they say something in the Bible about the bread for communion having to be without leaven?* Shrugging, I popped it into my mouth. "*Either I'm hungry, or this is the best bread I've ever had!*"

I looked at my son's reaction as he ate a piece. He nodded in approval as he passed the tray to the person beside him.

After another solemn prayer, more trays got passed around the sanctuary. This time, they held several tiny clear cups of water. I took a cup and drank. It went down smoothly.

Yeah, I'm hungry because this is the best water I've ever had!

We waited quietly for everyone to be served, the silence only pierced occasionally by coughs and whining toddlers. Once everyone had some, the boys gathered at the front of the sanctuary to return the used trays. Someone covered them with a white sheet, and the boys took a seat.

Three speakers spoke that day. One seemed to be hitting forty, one was a teenager, and another appeared to be in their sixties. The teenage girl with shiny black hair, piercing dark eyes, and impeccable style stood out. Her name was Grace, and she spoke about living her beliefs in her daily life. She used a lot of examples from her life at school, interactions with friends, and all kinds of things you would expect a young teen to talk about.

Sudden emotions overcame me, and I didn't know why. *Why am I about to cry? This speech is sweet with a child-like innocence. It's not as if she's getting into deep theology.* I chided myself, fighting back tears. I looked over at Pocket. His eyes welled with tears ready to fall over the lid.

It baffled me. *Why was what she said making us so emotional? I don't normally get that emotional.* It happened during a few breakups, the death of my father, fighting extreme suicidal ideation, or the turmoil of the psych ward, but it had to be something big.

Am I becoming an emotional wreck? Please God, anything but that.

6

THE BLESSING

I sat in my psychiatrist's lobby, staring at the jam-packed parking lot through big windows. The lobby overflowed with people from different programs offered by the psych ward. So many people, all waiting to be called somewhere: to class, to see the psychiatrist, or to get drug tested.

I arrived at my appointment 15 minutes early, but my psychiatrist was running late.

It's been over an hour and a half, and no one has come to get me yet. Nobody came to explain or apologize either. If I leave, they'll say I didn't show up and will send somebody to my home to pick me up.

Seriously, it's not fair. They can do whatever they want, and we can't say a thing. If you complain, you'll be labeled as emotional and dragged off to the psych ward. There's no choice but to put up with it.

Someone called my name, bringing me out of my thoughts.

"He's ready to see you." A petite staff member with straightened hair and a bright smile motioned for me to follow her down the hallway.

Hopping out of my chair, I quickly followed her. She walked briskly as she led me to a cracked door at the end of the hall, I could barely keep up. It creaked open. My psychiatrist wrote in a patient's file, greeting me without looking.

I handed my mood sheet to him as he closed the folder. Stacks of files covered his desk. *How many were there? Fifty? A hundred? That's not counting the four open dossiers whose papers intermingled.*

"So, tell me, how have things been going?" His head was still down as he pulled out a file that appeared to be mine and placed it on top of the open files.

"I guess it's been ok. Just trying to get this weight off." *The medication caused me to gain even more weight as time progressed. It hurts to exercise, and with the extra pounds, I become winded quickly.* "Is there anything else I can take? This is affecting my ability to work."

"Hmmm." He flipped through my file. "Well, you've been on this a while. Does it feel like it's helping?"

"Not really."

He looked at me. "Let's try this one more month, and then we can talk about putting you on something else. Okay?"

"Okay." I nodded, biting my lip. *I wish I could quit this medication right now. This weight gain is becoming a real pain. Pain, swelling, hemorrhaging, and other difficulties related to* my sickness last longer because of it. Also, I feel more depressed because I don't like what I look like in the mirror. The psych ward saved my life, but they also ruined it.

He studied my file. "What extracurricular activities are you doing? Getting out in the community? Meeting new people?"

I hesitated, not wanting to tell him about the church yet. "I'm trying different stuff. Putting myself out there." As an afterthought, I shared something more personal. "I've made two new friends." *He doesn't need to know that they're sister missionaries.*

"Good! Keep it up!" He closed my file.

I looked at my phone. It had only been four minutes.

He pulled out a prescription pad and started writing. "Still suffering from anxiety too?"

"Yes." I exhaled deeply.

"Great seeing you today." He handed me a prescription. "Keep up the good work. I'll see you in four weeks."

I headed for the door, glancing back as I reached for the door handle.

His head was back down, and he was writing fervently into another file. "Leave the door open."

"Okay." I slipped out of the room fuming. *After waiting an hour and a half, I get 4 minutes? How can you possibly evaluate someone's mental health in that amount of time? I suppose I should be grateful that I even got that.*

This guy is responsible for patients on the mod, people in the outpatient programs, and those who graduated but still get medication management.

I need a new psychiatrist.

My phone dinged as I exited the hospital. *The missionaries sent me a message.*

"Hey! We were thinking about having our lesson at the Church tonight. Would you all be able to meet there for the lesson at 6:15 pm?"

Oh, God. What's going to happen next? Lessons always took place at our house. I'm not up for any surprises.

I controlled my breathing, and my hands shook as I carefully typed each letter. "Ok. We can meet at the church … Is this a siege? I mean, what should we expect?"

They responded with a laughing-crying face emoji. "No. We just thought it would be fun to switch it up!"

I'm still not sure about this. "Okay. Yeah, we'll be there."

• • •

Pocket and I each sat on one of the five hard metal folding chairs that the missionaries placed in the vestibule of the empty sanctuary. I huffed. *Theo dodged the appointment at the last minute.* The two of them sat across from us, smiling reassuringly and bowing their heads to pray.

Although the missionary prayed in her regular speaking voice, her voice had no echo. It stayed muted in the circle, making the huge empty sanctuary seem creepy. Goosebumps formed on my arms as I hugged myself.

"… In the name of Jesus Christ, Amen." Her head popped up, and she smiled knowingly.

Their idea of switching it up was to introduce what they called The Word of Wisdom.

Not sure I'd call this fun. So if I got this right, it's a bunch of strong suggestions. You don't have to do them, but there may be repercussions within the church if you don't.

They handed us a pamphlet with bullet points based on a chapter in another book that church members read. It listed foods good for the body, such as fruits and wholesome herbs and vegetables, sparingly eating meat, and grains such as wheat, rice, and oats.

That's cool. I need to eat better anyway.

"These are substances that we can't have according to the Word of Wisdom because they aren't good for you." One of the missionaries spoke as I read the pamphlet.

"No alcohol…"

Ouch. But I don't drink that much anymore, so I guess that's fine.

"No tobacco…"

That might be a challenge. I glanced at Pocket, who raised his eyebrows and lowered his head laughing.

"…and no tea or coffee."

I shook my head. "I've been drinking coffee since I was like twelve or thirteen years old! There's no way I'm going to stop drinking it." *Plus, even if he's quiet now, Pocket loves sweet tea. Following the Word of Wisdom would take an act of God.*

"Well, you don't have to decide right now. Take some time to think about it."

The sisters shared rules that they called laws to follow as well. One stood out: The Law of Chastity.

"How are we supposed to follow the law of chastity if we have already had sex and have a normal sex life?" I raised an eyebrow.

The two missionaries blushed, causing them to look their young age.

They glanced at each other, and then one spoke with a wince. "You'll have to try to be celibate."

"What! I'm not doing that!" My eyes widened.

"Well, otherwise, you'll have to move into separate houses."

I laughed. *Seriously? I can't believe this.* "You don't know what it is to break up a home. To live in two separate places, you have to pay two separate home expenses and break up our children..." I counted each item on my fingers.

One of them shrugged. "I know it'll be hard, but-"

"I'm not doing it." I shook my head vehemently.

They traded glances and nodded. "Once again, you don't have to decide right now. Just think about it. Read the pamphlet, and if you have any questions, you can text us."

I looked at the paper and gripped it tightly. *It wouldn't look good if I crumpled it and threw it in their faces.* I gritted my teeth. "Okay." Then, remembering that I was in a church and should be reverent, I smiled.

They're going to have to baptize me while I'm a full sinner because there is no way that I'm going to be celibate.

"You could also get married..." One spoke softly.

Married?!

I'm happy with the way our relationship is. Our previous marriages were disastrous. Pocket and I have been together for several years now, and we get along great. We never fight, listen to each other, and know how to work together. Free to stay and free to leave if it's not working without bankrupting ourselves. How could I ask for anything more? What if doing so would ruin what we have? What's that saying? 'If it ain't broke don't fix it.' Things are perfect the way they are.

Besides, there's a major problem. We're both still married to our exes. I'm not ready to face my ex in court. A former military officer, he was abusive, controlling, and overall toxic. The thought alone terrifies me.

My breathing quickened and my palms became sweaty.

Plus Pocket's ex has a right to half of his money, including his retirement, and paying her off is already draining his accounts. Adding child support on top of everything would be the last nail in the coffin, ruining him financially.

I know it, and it doesn't bother me while he's my partner... but to have another broke husband? I can't do that again. We can't both be broke, it wouldn't work. I definitely won't think about marriage until he's back on his feet.

These sister missionaries are too young to understand what their suggestions entail or how hard it is. They lack life experience. Wait a few more years, kids, and let's see if you'll still say the same thing.

Pocket and I looked at each other anxiously. "I don't think we want to get married, per se..." I started.

"Well, think about what we discussed tonight, give it some time, and we can go from there."

We nodded, and they said a closing prayer.

This is going to be a quiet ride home.

● ○ ●

However, it wasn't a quiet ride home. It was night, and we were hungry after leaving the church, so we headed to a local chicken place to get something to eat.

On the way, we contemplated the pros and cons of getting married. *It isn't like we don't love each other. We just aren't in the right place in our lives to get married - even if we divorced our spouses.*

We were so deep in conversation that I hadn't realized that I brought The Book of Mormon into the restaurant with us. On auto-pilot, I placed it on our table.

"You brought The Book of Mormon?" Pocket laughed, raising his eyebrows.

I looked at the blue book, sitting on the table for all to see. "I guess so." I chuckled, shrugging as I grabbed it.

Maybe I should put it on the bench next to me. "You know what? I'll leave it here, and if somebody asks we can explain it to them." I waved my hand, putting it back down on the table.

Pocket shrugged his shoulders, still laughing. "Okay. I guess that's what we're doing then. We'll leave it out in the open for everyone to see!"

Nobody said anything, but many people in the restaurant walked past our table and looked at it. Whenever we caught someone looking, we smiled at them. *The night isn't a total bust, after all.*

• • •

The following Sunday, Pocket and I stood outside the church, bouncing slightly to stay warm. He lit up a cigarette. It looked as if I was smoking too, each time I exhaled.

Is he allowed to smoke right in front of the church? I looked around for an ashtray. "What kind of place doesn't have an outdoor ashtray!?" I swayed in the cold, rubbing my arms.

"I was like you." A robust man with tan skin and feathery gray hair stood a few feet away at the church entrance.

"What?" Pocket put out his cigarette and threw it on the ground.

"I was like you some time ago. I used to smoke too."

Pocket adjusted the cigarettes in his pocket as we made our way to the door.

"I smoked until the day I got baptized. I smoked a cigarette, threw it out, got baptized, and never smoked again." He held the door open for us.

Touching Pocket's arm, I lowered my voice. "That never happens." I slipped past the man.

For that to happen, it would take a miracle, and I'm a living witness that God doesn't do miracles. My heart broke all over again. *I thought I got better with the whole Jesus, God, and His love stuff, but what that guy said crushed my heart again. Why him and not me? What are the qualifications to receive a miracle?*

The robust man entered the crowded vestibule behind us.

"Patriarch Shim!" A tall, casually dressed gentleman with dark wavy hair squeezed past us.

Turning to see who he was talking to, I noticed it was the man who held the door open for us.

Patriarch? What does that mean? Does it mean he's the father of the church? I've heard of church mothers, but never a church father... I know that the church has many locations. Did he start the church at this location?

Pocket and I exchanged glances, and I mouthed: "What is a Patriarch?"

He shrugged. "The father of the church? I don't know..."

Making our way to the missionaries, we sat with them.

"We set it up so you can get your blessings today." They beamed.

"What do you mean? I don't want to be hexed by anyone." *Everyone's idea of a blessing is different.*

They smiled, shaking their heads. "You won't be hexed. There is just a group of men from the church that pray for you."

"Okay..." I eyed them suspiciously.

The rest of the hour was a blur. I didn't know who spoke or what went on. I vaguely remember taking part in the sacrament portion of the service. My mind was focused on the blessing that we would be given after.

Once the service ended, we followed the missionaries through the maze of church members in the hallway towards a small classroom where three older gentlemen stood around a single metal folding chair. Two of them I knew. Matthew White, the guy who came to our house with the missionaries that day, and Tim Guffey, the gentleman from Christmas festivities. The third, a gentleman with white hair and a jolly laugh, introduced himself as John Manwaring.

"You go first, in case something weird happens." *I'm only half-joking.*

The guys in the room chuckled and motioned for Pocket to sit in the chair.

Before I realized it, it was over. Pocket stood up to shake the men's hands, and then it was my turn.

I sat on the metal chair, and someone asked me for my full name. After giving it to them, someone standing behind me dripped a few small drops of anointing oil on the top of my head. Suddenly three sets of hands lightly pressed my crown. I closed my eyes. *This will be good to use for encouragement later on. I'm going to remember every part of this blessing.*

However, once they said amen, the prayer was completely erased from my mind.

We left the building feeling no different than when we went in. Nothing exciting happened. We just prayed and left.

Pocket lit his cigarette as we walked through the parking lot and took a deep drag. Quickly exhaling before he entered the car, he wrinkled his face in disgust. "This cigarette tastes funny."

I turned to look at him as he started the car. "I don't know why..."

He inhaled again, spitting out the smoke. "Ugh! It's disgusting!" He licked the steering wheel and his fist. "I can't get the taste out of my mouth!"

I rolled my eyes. "You're doing most of it!"

"I'm telling you, something's wrong with my cigarette!" He looked at me, eyes wide. "I smoked one from this pack before we went in. It was fine!"

"What do you think happened to it?" *He looks like he's going to cry.* I softened my attitude.

He threw the cigarette out of the window. "I don't know. This is a new pack…Nothing could have gotten to it because it was in my pocket the whole time. They never fell out or anything."

"I don't know what could have happened…" I shrugged helplessly.

Starting the car, he headed to a nearby restaurant, as per our new after-church custom on Sundays. Quiet and less than a block from the church, we get served immediately.

After pulling into the parking lot, Pocket took out another cigarette. I leaned against the car, while he lit up. He grimaced. "Ugh! It's even worse than the last one!" Throwing it on the ground, he stomped across the parking lot and into the restaurant.

We ate in silence. *The meal is as good as usual, but Pocket looks so frustrated. He really wants to smoke. I feel so bad for him.*

Packing our things, we left the restaurant. He lit up a cigarette on the way to the car. "Ugh! It's like melted wax all over my tongue!" He moaned in frustration. Turning around, he threw it away in the outdoor ashtray. Following behind him, I kept my distance, in case he would flip out. *I've never seen him like this. What do I do?*

"Babes, why continue to tempt God?" I inhaled in shock, clutching my neck. *Who said that?*

He turned to face me. "What?"

"Why tempt God?" I heard myself say again.

"I'm not tempting God! I just want a smoke and it tastes disgusting!"

I paused, softening my voice as much as I could. "What if He doesn't want you to smoke, and you keep trying?"

He stormed across the parking lot and got in the car.

We still spoke normally on the way back, but once home he stayed outside to try again.

"How can this cigarette taste even worse than the last one? Maybe it's a problem with the pack." He threw out the whole pack and marched over to where he kept his stash.

"What the…" Searching all over, he left a mess in his wake. "Where did they all go?"

No matter where he looked, all of his packs of cigarettes had disappeared. My thoughts kept going back to the gentleman who opened the door for us and the blessing ceremony. *Perhaps it's an act of God.*

"So … Pocket is at work, and he's a hot mess because he can't get any nicotine."

I texted the missionaries as tears ran down my face. *This is crazy. Not only is Pocket unable to smoke, but I've become so emotional and cry at the slightest things! Not just uncomfortable or bad things, but even happy or regular things, like discussing what's for dinner. Normally, I'm pretty detached, yet now I feel unhinged, and my heart aches so badly. It's like I'm crying for all the times in my life that I should have cried, but didn't. The blessing they gave us became a curse!*

"Every time he tries to smoke it tastes horrible to him, so he hasn't smoked today. Please pray for him and his withdrawal. This is the longest he has gone without, and he's very frustrated."

Blinking to clear my blurry vision, I clutched my phone tightly and stared at the screen.

"Oh my! We will definitely keep him in our prayers! Has he tried, like, nicotine gum or something like that?"

Ugh! So they don't have any answers for this? I tossed my phone onto the couch. *If God was responsible for what's happening to Pocket, I doubt nicotine gum would help. What kind of God gets rid of your cigarettes but doesn't get rid of your cravings?*

I wiped my tears away angrily. *And why is it that he gets this huge miracle, and I become a basket case? How unfair, it's like God loves him more. He could have at least gotten rid of my syndrome, but instead, he makes me cry?! This sucks.*

Two days later, I still cried for every little thing, and Pocket still struggled with nicotine withdrawal, causing emotions to fly high in our house. It scared our son. *Theo felt unsafe in the house, so he 'ran away'. Well, he's twenty years old, so he'll be fine. Besides, I don't have the mental capacity to help him right now, and neither does Pocket.*

I flopped onto the couch, texting the missionaries out of the blue, skipping the pleasantries.

"Pocket is really having a bad go about this cigarette thing. He hasn't been able to smoke since the blessing. He started to gag, choke, and almost vomit every time he wanted to smoke so he stopped trying. He says his cigarettes taste like dog**** now. And his withdrawals are making him very grouchy, but he can't smoke. He physically can't smoke. We never argue, like, ever. We always talk things out, and now it's like we can't even talk without snapping each other's heads off. *Sigh* Just pray."

Maybe they think I'm making a big deal out of this, or they don't have much experience with miracles, but nothing they say makes me feel any better. These so-called miracles are curses. I'd like to give them back so our lives can go back to normal.

"We're so sorry it's been hard! We'll be praying for you guys for sure. It's pretty common that when we make significant steps in the gospel, Satan tries to make it hard for us to progress. That's when we need to be the strongest. We know it's difficult, but we believe in you guys! Prayer is key!"

We've been praying, begging actually. If only all of this mayhem would stop. This whole blessing thing was a horrible idea. It was a trap. I don't think we can make it.

• • •

The following Sunday, I sat in the church sanctuary, fighting tears. There was no reason to cry. People sang a few hymns, none of which made a particular impact on me. I still couldn't stop crying.

I glanced around the church, looking for our son. Pocket and I made eye contact, and I shook my head. *I haven't seen him or heard from him in three days. He didn't even call, which isn't like him at all. I had hoped to see him here at the church. What if something happened to him?*

When the service ended, and the sanctuary was clearing out, we saw him in the back of the church talking to the Elders and other church members. The sister missionaries, who sat with us during service, hurried to greet him with a big smile.

Pocket and I hung around the benches where we sat during the service, watching our son interact with the people around him. I waved to get his attention. He made eye contact and looked away, going straight into another conversation with someone near him, without waving back.

I don't understand why he's angry with us. It's not like we did anything to him. Seriously, we had a normal life before this.

• • •

The next day, I felt better than all the previous days. Sitting on my knees in front of my bed, I texted the missionaries. "I've been crying on and off all day. I don't feel broken like I did yesterday. But I haven't cried like this since my dad died suddenly four years ago."

I closed my eyes, remembering that day. *It's been four years since that phone call. One of my younger brothers called me to tell me my dad was found dead on the bathroom floor. A lightning strike would have hurt less. The pain was unbearable. I screamed and cried. It felt like my heart would stop, and I couldn't breathe. To make the pain stop, I grabbed the nearest bottle of rum and drank straight from the bottle.*

Poor Pocket tried to hold me, but I was inconsolable.

I even yelled and cursed at the sky, hoping my dad would hear me. At the same time, I desperately wanted to know if my dad was okay where he was. Was he cold? Was he being comforted? Did he need anything?

Never have I felt anything like that in my life. Until I got this blessing from the church, that is.

"We're so sorry! Is there anything we can do for you at all? If you need people to talk to, we're always here!"

Contemplating their offer, I paused.

"I dunno what you can do. I guess it's part of the process. Just a ton of different feelings that I don't know what to do with. If it's still going on tomorrow, I'm going to have to see a professional because this is ridiculous."

They agreed. "It's part of the process and we know it will pass. God is aware of you and will help you along the way. We're always here for ya, only a text or call away! And that would be a good idea!"

Leaning my head against my bed, I considered praying. *I don't really want to get professional help. Telling my psychiatrist definitely won't do anything. He'll say I have a mood disorder or that I'm having a depressive episode, and if I start crying in his office, it'll be a one-way ticket back to the psych ward. On top of that, he'll increase the dose of the medication that I'm trying to get changed. I'll gain even more weight and be even more miserable.*

I closed my eyes to pray, then clicked my tongue. *It happened again. Praying in my head was difficult. Every time I talk to God about something, a memory would pop up in my mind, completely unrelated, and interrupt my train of thought.* Refocusing, I tried to pick up where I left off. *Great. Now another voice is throwing out suggestions and topics in the middle of my prayer. How am I supposed to focus like this?*

Sighing, I lifted my eyes to the ceiling. "You know what I'm trying to say. In Jesus' name, Amen."

I'll try again tomorrow.

• • •

After reading the Book of Mormon for a few weeks, I made it to Alma, which is about halfway. Suddenly, I stopped reading, fixated on the scripture that I just read.

"Blessed be the name of our God; let us sing to his praise, yea, let us give thanks to his holy name, for he doth work righteousness forever."

For some reason, I felt strange, like a warm blanket enveloped me. I stopped to contemplate the cause of the sudden onset of warmth and giddiness. Then, like when Pocket tried to smoke in the restaurant parking lot, a thought popped into my mind and came out of my mouth before I could stop it.

"I'm not suicidal anymore..." I whispered to myself in surprise.

How can that be? I've been struggling with suicidal thoughts since I was a kid. After spending the first six or seven years of my life in the hospital, I was even part of a hospital schooling program where teachers came directly to the hospital to teach kids with long-term and terminal illnesses. No one ever thought about how it would affect me mentally and emotionally. Kids are resilient, they said.

Even when a child is in constant pain, watching their friends in the hospital die overnight, and – if lucky enough to get out for a few weeks – is bullied by kids at school for being different.

Nobody cared to know or look too closely.

I tried to die so many times, and whenever I didn't try, I wanted to. At forty years old, with many failed suicide attempts under my belt, I still wanted to commit suicide. You're telling me I'm done with that now? Me?

It felt like a weight was lifted off of my shoulders. "I'm not suicidal?" I asked myself out loud.

I looked around to see if anyone could hear me. It was as if a voice spoke, inside and outside of my body simultaneously. "You're not suicidal anymore."

I smiled, giggling to myself, and accepted it. "Okay." I marveled. "I'm not suicidal anymore."

No fanfare and no angel lighting up the living room where I was sitting. Nothing spectacular happened, and there were no witnesses except God and Jesus Christ.

I'm healed. It's truly a miracle.

7

NEW FRIENDS

After a couple of weeks had passed, things started to go back to normal.

Pocket peeked into the living room. "You feeling any better?"

"Yeah, it's safe." I smirked, my legs resting on the couch. *My crying spell finally ended.* "What about you?"

"I still think about smoking, but I don't feel like I'm niccing anymore. Every time I think of cigarettes, I remember that taste again, and I want to vomit!"

"Well, don't do that!" I gave him a small smile.

Plopping down onto the couch, he moved my legs to his lap. "Did Theo ever tell you why he was mad at us?"

I shrugged. "He said that I scared him. He's never seen me like that, so he feared for his safety."

Pocket scrunched his eyebrows. "That doesn't make sense."

"We were kind of wild."

Suddenly, it was quiet as we were both in our thoughts.

"The missionaries are coming to teach us tonight." *I want our conversation to last a little longer.*

Nodding, he rubbed the back of my legs, massaging my calves absentmindedly.

There was another silence.

"I'm done reading the Book of Mormon. I mean, I finished it." I poked his side.

Snapping out of his thoughts, he turned to look at me, eyes wide. "That was fast! I haven't even started yet!"

"Not at all?" I chuckled.

"Nothing!"

I roared with laughter. "That's messed up! So that's why you're so quiet when the missionaries ask questions!"

He shrugged sheepishly while laughing. "You've read enough for both of us."

I looked down at my phone. "That reminds me. I need to tell the missionaries that I finished."

"So … I completed the Book of Mormon yesterday and began the Doctrine & Covenants. I have questions about the Lamanites who believed in Christ and changed their names. They disappear from the storyline completely. What happened to them?"

The girls responded swiftly. "We don't know exactly what happened to them, but everyone who wasn't a Lamanite was killed."

Furrowing my brow, I stared intently at my phone. "Later in the book those Lamanites who believed joined the Nephites and became fair like them (even their wives and daughters), but they didn't change their names?"

Pocket slid my legs aside so that he could get up.

"You're leaving?" I pouted.

"I'll be back in time for the missionaries." Chuckling, he kissed my forehead and disappeared into the hallway.

Remembering that I was texting, I looked at my phone. The missionaries had responded.

"The Lamanites who became righteous and joined the Nephites just call themselves "Nephites." They became "fair" when they repented, and the "curse" was lifted. This is symbolic. It mentions skins becoming white, but they didn't actually turn white. Their countenances became white, like the Light of Christ. This also makes it clear that having dark skin is not a curse at all."

I should probably wait until our next lesson, but I can't. As soon as I read their text, my fingers moved in a flurry across my screen.

"Even though the Nephites waiver, they still come out as believers. By the time you get to the 3rd section, the Lamanites are still listed along with the Ishmaelites as unbelievers. The Lamanites seem to be perpetually cast as those who need salvation. I need help because the Book of Mormon establishes the race of the Lamanites early on as dark (remember I questioned that?).

I'm dark so, in the generalized sense of the Lamanites being black, I can relate to that. But, I struggle with it being a curse.

And the Lamanites constantly being stigmatized, even

though they do the same thing as the Nephites (who appear to get their punishment and repent in cycles, but are not stigmatized), is disheartening - but I'll keep reading because maybe my questions will be answered later."

I'm sure that the missionaries are tired of my long messages. Maybe I should send them an email. Do they even have regular access to a computer? Biting my bottom lip, I twirled my hair around my finger.

It wasn't long before another text came, like a mini-lesson in my inbox.

"When they talk about the Nephite believers, they're referring to those who kept the records which are the Book of Mormon (Nephi, Jacob, Enos, Alma, etc). About the D&C, the records kept by the Nephites, Jacobites, Josephites, and Zoramites (all killed because everyone was wicked in the end) were brought forth and translated by Joseph Smith.

Those records kept by the ancient prophets are the Book of Mormon. The purpose of the Book was to return the info to the Lamanites (who would eventually repent again). They "dwindle in unbelief" not because they were necessarily wicked but because their fathers never taught them the gospel. Enos asks God to preserve their records for the future benefit of the Lamanites."

The missionaries are young but well-educated. They probably read the whole Book of Mormon multiple times. No matter what I ask, they have the answer. It's reassuring that they're patient and not defensive.

They taught my family and me out of a book called 'Preach My Gospel', a book teaching how to self-study as well as teach others, but our questions touched more profound matters. The lessons ended up going into deep doctrine. *I don't want any surprises. If they want us to get baptized at the church, we need to know more than surface-level stuff. Baptism is a serious matter for our family, so they better bring their A-game.*

● ● ●

Theo, Pocket, and I stood in the hallway of a young couple's house. *The missionaries said they would be cool to get to know.* When the couple invited the missionaries over for dinner, somehow we got to tag along.

How does such a young couple get a house this nice? Surveying the main floor of their beautiful two-story home, with a sunken living room, and kitchen complete with a double farmhouse sink, I felt a familiar feeling of sadness.

Another person who has the life I want, but can never have. I want to leave.

Jake was a tall, dark, and handsome man. He had mischievous brown eyes and an all-American smile, appearing to be in his late twenties or early thirties. His wife Courtney was a petite, athletically shaped brunette and looked to be in her mid to late twenties. With two little girls and a baby boy, they looked like the poster family for The Church of Jesus Christ of Latter-Day Saints.

She's beautiful! How do you have three kids and still look that good? I'm still trying to lose "baby weight" from twenty years ago!

I smiled brightly, stifling my emotions.

They weren't the only people from the church we visited.

Thanks to the missionaries, we went to several members' homes because we were new, yet regular, visitors to the church.

They said people wanted to get to know us.

I don't get it. Every time we visit a church member, it's crazy how big a house they own, and at such a young age. Five-bedroom homes, at least three bathrooms, full basements, and built-in in-law suites… Whatever a person could desire, their houses had it. They must be worth half a million. Only a handful of them were under three hundred thousand.

Our house is less than a hundred thousand dollars.

We don't belong in this church. I followed the group to Jake and Courtney's dining room. *I'll tell the missionaries: 'Thanks, but I don't think we're a good fit.' Everyone in this church is rich.*

Making my way around their living room table to find a seat, I tried to make eye contact with Pocket and Theo.

It felt like we were charity cases. I think missionaries should introduce prospective members who are on the lower end financially to people in the church who are more like them, living the same kind of lifestyle. Once they're hooked, then you can introduce them to those with an inspirational lifestyle.

It lowers the barrier to entry, and they can see themselves being members of the church because they were first introduced to people like them. We met one young couple living in an apartment coming closer to our situation, but they could have been our kids.

It's making us doubt if we should become members or not.

I can't see my family among such wealthy people in our current condition. The church was rich, so what did they want us for?

Once everyone was seated, they brought in a huge crockpot full of pulled pork accompanied by nachos, buns, and some sides. My family and I were about to start making sandwiches when we noticed Jake and Courtney bowing their heads to pray for the food.

Oops... Holding back smiles, we exchanged looks and respectfully waited for the prayer to end.

Pocket, seated on my right, leaned over. "I'm starting to think this is probably a cult. Don't get caught up in it."

I glanced at him with my head down. "Me too. Why do you?"

"Because they're too nice."

Everyone we've met is too nice. "Maybe ... the missionaries do dress funny..."

We scooted closer to the table and prepared our plates.

● ● ●

Although we went in leaning heavily on the missionaries for support, we lost track of them and time.

Jake leaned forward, "So Pocket, what do you do?"

Pocket hesitated momentarily. "I work in a test lab. We test parts and things for large companies to ensure they're safe for public use."

Jake nodded and raised his eyebrows.

They started talking about their jobs and what sounded like mechanical parts in their line of work. *I'm lost. I don't know what any of that stuff means.*

Smiling at Courtney, I raised my eyebrows. *I wonder if she knows what they're talking about.*

She smiled. *I don't get how she does it. She looks calm. Well, as calm as you can be when wrangling three kids.*

"What about you, Theo?" Jake turned his attention toward my son, who was at the head of the table.

"I sell life insurance. So, I work for myself."

That's a stretch. Pocket and I are his only customers. He mostly added people to his 'team'. Insurance is his second job. Why wouldn't he just say he is a barista at a coffee shop? That's the whole truth. What's wrong with being a barista?

I snapped out of my thoughts in time to hear Jake ask me about myself.

"I'm a commercial, TV, and film actor."

"So I should get your autograph." He winked.

I chuckled. *Don't get my autograph. At the rate things are going, it won't be worth anything.* "I've been in a few films with A-listers but only in small parts with a few lines. Most of my work was regional." *Although I have wanted to act since I was a little girl, I'm picky about the jobs I select.*

After several minutes of conversation, I smiled slowly. *What warm and cheerful people. Everyone seems to be having fun. Their kids are so inquisitive and well-behaved. It feels like we're part of the family.*

• • •

Once we finished our meals, Jake offered a small selection of board games to play.

We don't know any of these. Maybe playing board games isn't such a good idea. I don't do well in competitive situations. Pocket and Theo will probably want to play though, so I guess I should too. If it gets too stressful, I'll make a break for the toilets.

"Have you ever played this game before?" Jake handed out small books with whiteboard-like materials and markers.

"We don't know about any games at all." My cheeks flushed red. *I feel embarrassed.*

"It's okay. All you have to do is …"

• • •

The game ended, and the missionaries announced that they were leaving, so we all got up to see them out.

"Have you met the Ashfords yet?" Sister Robison smiled.

"Oh! Yeah, you've got to meet them. They're so great!" Courtney practically glowed.

"Uhhh…" I thought about all of the people we met so far. "I don't think so."

Courtney's smile widened. "You're going to love them! We'll get you in touch with them."

I leaned against the wall. "That'll be good. We're still trying to make friends."

"So many people want to get to know you guys!" Sister Robison went on. "Is that okay?"

I could feel my chest tightening as memories from the Christmas event came flooding back. "Yeah." I tried to inhale normally so they wouldn't notice I was having trouble breathing. "That'll be great!" I smiled weakly.

Pocket looked at me from the corner of his eye with an eyebrow raised. I felt his hand on my shoulder.

"Okay! This will be great." Courtney gushed.

The room started to spin, and I felt the blood drain from my face. *I've got to get out of here and sit down.* I checked out, trying to maintain my composure. *Just keep smiling.*

I heard everyone, including myself, saying their goodbyes. *Did we hug? What's going on?* My body was on autopilot. Suddenly, the cool air outside hit me as we stepped onto their porch. My ears were ringing.

Pocket led me to the car, opened the door, and helped me in.

My legs were weak and, though it was cool outside, I was sweating. I leaned my head against the headrest. "I like them." I slurred deliriously.

Pocket and Theo nodded.

Now I have friends from the church who aren't missionaries.

• • •

The church had a study book called 'Come Follow Me', and we would go to Jake and Courtney's house to study it with them. Rather, they taught us from it.

I'm really thankful. Even though I finished reading The Book of Mormon, there are still so many things I don't understand about it or the doctrine of the church itself.

What is the Priesthood? Why do only men and boys get the Priesthood, and women only have 'access' to it? Why can only men give blessings? It doesn't seem right. It's like women are second-class citizens in the church.

And why should only the President of the church get prophetic revelations?

If God reveals something to regular people without a title, it isn't their fault - and they shouldn't disobey if He does.

I sighed, shaking my head.

They told me many times, but I still don't get most of it. The sister missionaries explained that the President, or Prophet, gets revelation on how to run the church and we get revelations on how to run ourselves and our family.

After a while, Courtney and Jake began to teach us straight from The Book of Mormon instead of "Come Follow Me. They even gave us all engraved quads that contained The Book Of Mormon, The Pearl Of Great Price, The Bible, and The Doctrine and Covenants.

We're not even baptized, and they're giving us so many things. I learn even more from them than I do the missionaries! It's like they're preparing us to get baptized.

Sighing, I sat on the edge of my bed.

It's not like I'm not ready to accept what Jesus did for us on the cross or follow him for life; it's just that I can't right now.

Neither Pocket nor I will be getting baptized anytime soon or following the covenant path, because we're still married to other people. People have to either be single or married to their current partner to get baptized. That's definitely not us.

Falling backward, I stared at the plaster on the ceiling.

Even the way we met wasn't conventional. I smiled, remembering the day I signed up for the app. *Twenty-four hours after creating my account, my inbox got flooded by over two hundred men asking for a date. It was crazy and a bit overwhelming.*

I set up dates with the only two people whose vocabulary

wasn't limited to 'hey baby' and 'you're so hot' and who seemed a little more than just physically attracted to me. At least they actually read my profile.

The first guy was a chef for a five-star restaurant in the city, and the other was Pocket, a blue-collar guy at that time. In a way, it was like a blind date, because I didn't even see his pictures before going out with him due to the flood of responses.

We were complete opposites.

He came from the country, and I came from the city; he was white, and I was black; he is healthy, I'm sickly; I had enough religious experience to know that I was agnostic, and he had no experience and was an atheist.

As my username ended in saurus, he jumped into my in-box with a play on words. 'Are you a carnivore, omnivore, or herbivore?'

I laughed. *What a way to break the ice.*

Twirling one of my dark, fluffy curls around my finger, I smiled.

Our date took place at a bar. We drank beer and talked like we had known each other forever. We even forgot to order food. He was upfront. After he explained he was married but separated, I confessed I was too. I felt relieved that he was okay with it and understood.

After the date, he asked me for a kiss goodbye. I normally never kiss on the first date, but this time I hesitated. Then I figured that as a wife and mother, there's no virtue left to save. So I kissed him.

It's a good thing I did, because he later told me that if I didn't, that would have been the last time we saw each other.

Our relationship moved faster than I expected.

I told him he had to meet my dog and only if she liked him could we date. She's picky about men. But not only did she like him, she begged for belly rubs. Well, it was a good thing they got along so well. A few weeks later, my dad died suddenly, and Pocket volunteered to watch her while Theo and I traveled back to the East Coast.

My smile faded at the memory of my dad passing away as tears welled up. I sat up quickly, blinking to remove the excess liquid and pushing the thought away.

After a year together, we moved in with each other, still not divorced yet.

Divorce is expensive. Who has the money? We didn't mind, because our relationship was great and neither of us wanted to get married again. Rather than going through the hassle, we figured we could just live together forever. That is, until five years later, when the missionaries came into our lives with The Book of Mormon.

I'm no novice when it comes to the bible, so I peppered them with advanced questions. Funnily enough, those young missionaries didn't feel intimidated. Even when Sister Robison got a new partner, they knew their stuff and how to teach it. They charged ahead, not even hesitating when they learned they'd have to help me untangle my life from my ex for me to get baptized.

My phone dinged, snapping me out of my thoughts. I scrambled across the bed to the side table.

"Hi! We were wondering how things are looking with the divorce finalization and wedding plans! If you have anything planned, Bishop Ashford can marry you for free."

I adore the Ashford family, so much so that I arbitrarily claim them as friends. Bishop Ashford is very approachable. We even played board games together. His wife, Trisha, is one of the best cooks I know. Not to mention his daughters make those amazing brownies.

Pocket and I wouldn't trust anyone else to marry us ... if we could ever get divorced.

"I have a confidential address hearing on March 23 at 9 a.m. (because my ex is pretty dangerous, and I don't want him to get my address off the divorce papers.) They are serving him by publication. So if he doesn't respond by the 28th of March, I'm supposed to have the Divorce Decree signed by the judge, and then it's all done. (At least that's how the case manager explained it). Please pray that it goes swiftly without any problems. I really want it to be done in time for baptism."

● ∘ ●

"Hi cutie!"

The infectious laugh hit me as soon as I opened the front door. It was Trisha Ashford with her two adorable blond girls on either side of her. Her blue eyes sparkled.

She seems awfully excited.

"We made you some brownies." The little one flashed me a smile as bright as her mother's.

Should I let them in? I glanced behind me to check the living room. *Too messy and small for this many people and my family.* I stepped onto the front stoop.

"Oh my gosh!" I gushed. "I love brownies!" *I mean, I adore brownies! They are my everything.*

Trisha handed me the plate. "We wanted you to know that we were thinking of you." She raised her eyebrows. "How are you doing?"

Since she knows about the divorce situation, she's probably not asking directly because she doesn't want her kids to know. I took the hint. "Everything is moving along. Still a lot of work to do." I attempted to be vague, but I was out of practice. *My kids are practically grown.*

Nodding, she put a hand on my arm. "Well, if you need anything, anything at all cutie, you give us a call, or text, or come by - whatever you need to do!" She smiled widely.

Is she serious, or is she being nice?

"I'm serious."

Did she read my mind?

"We're right here if you need us." Trisha opened her arms for a hug.

Not really a hugger, but ... I fell into her arms. *This isn't so bad.* I smiled.

I hugged her daughters as well, and then watched them walk across the yard. They turned one more time to wave goodbye. After they were out of sight, I closed the front door.

As I went to the kitchen to put the brownies away, I rubbed my temple. *Everything is so overwhelming. Why did I even try to do all this by myself? I need a lawyer. I can't do this alone.*

I grabbed a brownie. *I'm supposed to save this for later, but I need a pick-me-up right now.* I bit into it. *Mmmmm! Chocolatey!*

It's too bad, but I can't afford a lawyer. The missionaries help me stay motivated and do some of the legwork when I'm too sick to do so, but is it really enough? I hope it is. It has to be.

Another bite of the delicious brownie brought my mood right back up. *Let's look on the bright side; I've got a whole church supporting me. There's power in numbers, right?*

Everything seemed to be humming along until COVID-19 hit.

8

COVID-19

The day after delivering my special homemade chicken noodle soup, I stared out of our kitchen window as I cleaned the pan.

This is so weird. How many people does that make now? A lot of people have been sick lately. Supposedly, this sickness makes it extremely hard to breathe. They said it felt like the flu but ten times worse.

My chicken noodle soup usually works wonders. Whenever I or anyone else has had that soup, we're better in twenty-four hours. Neither my soup nor any medication seems to work.

This one lady was sick for over a month, and a friend of my family even died from it. The doctors think it's the flu, or pneumonia, or something.

On Sundays, I would look around the church benches and notice people missing for several weeks on end. Everyone I asked gave the same answer. *They have a bad cold. There's to be an awful lot of that going around lately.*

Then the announcement from the government came. *I should have followed the news. Why didn't I look into it more seriously before?*

The missionaries delivered more bad news.

"Hi! So we've been told to self-quarantine and won't be able to hold the lesson tonight. We should still be able to come to the baptism and sacrament at Jake and Courtney's, but if it's something that can be rescheduled we've been told to do so. If you want, we can Facetime or something, but we're supposed to stay home as much as we can!"

The church mandated that every house with a Priesthood holder has sacrament at home instead of going to church every Sunday. We don't have a Priesthood holder in our house. We're going to Jake and Courtney's for BOM club anyway, so let's have sacrament there.

But nothing went as expected. Everything shut down for a month. No one was allowed to go to church or leave their home. The church started having Sacrament, Relief Society, Elders Quorum, and Gospel Doctrine classes over Zoom.

We can't see Jake and Courtney at all now.

The terms of this lockdown keep changing. At first, they said two weeks. Then, it's not a full lockdown, but only a certain number of people can gather. How can people adapt and make plans when it keeps yo-yoing like this?

At least Pocket gets to stay home from work for a month. We'll get to spend lots of quality time together.

The grocery stores were packed. People pushed around carts filled so high its contents were practically spilling out.

They're buying everything. Shouldn't everyone at least share? Some people get everything, and some get nothing. Many people, like us, use napkins, baby wipes, and even coffee filters as emergency toilet paper because there's none left in the stores.

I ordered food and other necessary items online.

At least the delivery drivers are still making deliveries. This is crazy. A four-pack of toilet paper is going for up to twenty-two dollars. People have no choice but to order online though, since the stores are empty. On top of that, the news is saying that people are dying by the thousands. It's terrifying.

"You're buying too many groceries, babes." Pocket dragged the groceries from our front step into the house. "There's nowhere to put them all."

"Well, things are running out, so I have to get them when I can find them. Plus, I want to make sure we have enough food to eat." I pouted.

He looked around. "We have enough."

"Nobody knows when this thing will be over." I unpacked a grocery bag. "I should have listened better when we went to the emergency preparedness meeting the church had."

I bought as much as I could afford after the meeting, but it could only last us maybe two months. *It might not be enough.* "We need more money."

Pocket makes decent money, but between my hospital bills and his child support payments, even adding my on-again-off-again actor jobs sometimes barely gets us through the month.

I tried tithing and gave away a percentage of my wages. But rather than blessings and things working out, it felt like life got harder. Things wouldn't have been so desperate if I kept the money instead.

"Babes." He turned my face towards his. "I know you think this is the apocalypse, but we'll be ok. You've got frozen meat here and downstairs in the small freezer."

"But you never know. What if we have to barter and exchange to get something we need, or get locked in here for months and run out of food!" My eyes opened wide. "We gotta be ready for anything." *I made Pocket pick up a bunch of charcoal in case the gas and electricity go off and we can't cook on the stove; and ordered water.*

I handed Pocket the pack of water bottles. The stacks were too high now for me to put more on top. Quickly, I went to get another one, but even staying busy couldn't ward off the constant worries.

What if my son can't get baptized? They won't reschedule it, will they?

• • •

A few days later, as I was making dinner, a text message came in. I reached for my cell phone, putting down the spatula. It was the missionaries.

"Okay, so we were told that the people attending Theo's baptism should be limited to immediate family now, so just you and Pocket."

I held my breath as I read.

"We're so sorry. The virus is making everything so hard. So I guess your sister Apriel, and your friend can't come anymore." They added a bunch of sad-faced emojis.

"Oh! But Apriel is his aunt. Is that close enough? My friend is his godmother so I get it, they don't share blood." I refused to exhale as if holding my breath would make my sister and friend be allowed to go.

"Hmmm … Let's see if we can pull some strings and get permission for both of them to come. But they said absolutely no kids, so your niece and nephew can't come. Will that be a problem?

"No. That's fine." Finally exhaling, I lifted my eyes to the sky.

"Ok! Let's call the bishop real quick."

I said a silent prayer and stirred the food. *God, my sister really wants to come. Please, allow it to be so!*

For fifteen minutes, it was like time stood still. I kept looking at my phone, waiting for a message. My phone dinged. *I don't think a notification has ever sounded so good.*

"He said Apriel and your friend can come!"

I breathed a sigh of relief and thanked them for their efforts.

● ● ●

Pocket, Apriel, my friend, and I sat in a makeshift row of chairs inside the baptismal room. The room would normally be small, but today, with only ten people, it seemed large. It engulfed our small crowd.

In the back of the room, the pianist practiced a couple of hymns as we waited for the program to start. I noticed my sister staring ahead of her and tried to follow her line of sight to see what she was looking at. *She's staring at nothing!*

I leaned towards her with a fake excited smile. "Are you excited?"

She smiled at me lazily. "Yeah, are you?"

Not really. "Yeah." *After all this studying, making friends, and prepping for baptism, I still don't know if we should join this church, or not. I want to, but I'm having pre-baptism jitters.*

The baptism program started, and Sister Squire walked to the front of the room to conduct the music.

Are they actually going to have her stand up and conduct like they do the choir on Sundays for five people? I looked at the printout of the program. It had been left for attendees on a small end table next to a plate of Courtney's freshly baked cookies. *Courtney is outside in the parking lot with her kids, waiting for the ceremony to end so we can all take pictures together.*

Just baptize him, and let's get out of here. This is too much!

I wanted my family to get baptized, but I didn't know that we'd need a whole church service to get it done.

The singing of the hymns was so soft that we could barely hear her voice over the piano. I looked around the room.

We don't know these songs, and we outnumber the members.

I traded awkward glances with my friend. Her teeth were set on edge, which almost made me laugh. To stop myself from laughing at the ridiculousness of it all, I focused on the program in my hands.

After a while, we saw Jake step into the baptismal pool.

That's interesting. There's a giant slanted mirror above the pool. I chuckled. *Okay, stop nit-picking. Just enjoy the service.*

Theo entered from the side of the pool, wearing a pure white jumpsuit. *That looks like a painter's suit.*

I leaned over, whispering to Apriel and my friend. "Don't forget to take photos." *So much for keeping it down. I'm sure everyone heard that because the crowd is so small.*

The three of us whipped out our phones and took photos without the flash to not disturb the process. Before we knew it, Theo came out of the water, and he headed to the changing room to dry off and put on regular clothes.

The program continued as I swiped through the photos I had taken, only half paying attention to the rest.

After Theo changed, he came back to the room where we were all waiting.

On his way in, he grabbed a cookie and was still eating when they took him to a seat to pray over him. Luckily he finished it before they started. *The cookies were for after the ceremony, but he didn't know. Thankfully, they let it slide.*

The ceremony ended, so we all went outside to take pictures. Theo talked with the missionaries, cracking jokes to make them laugh.

That seems to be one of his favorite things to do.

I'm glad that Theo isn't disappointed that he couldn't invite more people. On the contrary, considering he dislikes crowds and gets nervous when put on the spot, this was right up his alley. I took several photos. *He looks happy. It's our church's first COVID-style baptism.*

• • •

"This will take longer than I thought. The judge won't grant me the confidential address and told me to find a lawyer because of the type of divorce I'm getting. And he couldn't set a final date thanks to COVID-19. I don't know any affordable divorce lawyers." Tears filled my eyes. *I don't get it. My ex is dangerous, but I can't get a confidential address granted. He rolled me up in a mattress and tried to suffocate me. This is how people end up being seriously hurt by their abusers.*

Ughhhh! ... I think there's actually a bishop who's a divorce lawyer. We'll look into it."

I'm grateful to have the missionaries on my side. Thankfully, they're open-minded.

Over the next few months, the missionaries helped me meet all the requirements to divorce someone when you don't know where they live. They made an exhaustive list of places and people to call, with addresses and phone numbers attached, to help provide proof to the court that I tried to contact him and couldn't find him.

We separated years ago. I don't really want to find him. Is it too much to ask for him to not answer the phone or be in police custody? At least then the court would consider him located and he would have to attend the divorce hearing. Even the thought of sharing a Zoom call with him is too much. I started hyperventilating. and my palms grew sweaty.

The missionaries found a potential address, so I mailed divorce papers there.

Getting divorced is hard enough as it is, but this pandemic is raising the bar. Offices operate at weird hours and are short-staffed. Even the mail comes twice a week instead of every day. On top of that, the courthouse no longer allows walk-ins. Instead of dropping off paperwork, I have to mail it.

I sealed the envelope for the courthouse.

Here's to hoping. I've lost count of how many times we've gone back and forth now. Each time I think I'm done and wait for good news, I get a nasty surprise three weeks later when I'm asked for clarification, a statement, or even notified that I forgot to write my name somewhere.

This is going to take forever.

The missionaries scheduled Zoom meetings with us a couple of times a week. *These girls help us stay sane. I'm so grateful that they're doing this much for us. Technically we're not even members yet since we haven't been baptized.*

Checking in regularly, the missionaries sent us another message. "How are you guys doing?"

Pocket and I had been sitting in the living room playing with our phones for the last few hours.

It has already been a week since the lab where he worked shut down. The news says a lot of couples argue and even break up during confinement because they can't take being around their partner all the time without an outlet. Thankfully Pocket and I don't have that problem. When we hang out together, we have fun, and even when we need a break, we still want to be in the same room.

The boredom is getting to us both, though.

"Doing pretty good today. Boredom comes in waves. Been trying to keep myself busy. Worked out today." I added the muscle emoji.

"Would you guys like to have a lesson over Zoom tonight?"

I feel like I'm drowning in stress. "Yes! We need a lesson. Possibly on patience, perseverance, or faith. Whatever will motivate us through this crisis. Come armed with testimonies because Pocket learns by hearing stories."

"We're about to go work out too! Maybe play some tennis? Then we'll get the lesson ready!"

"I don't know what we would do without the missionaries." I looked at Pocket, who was sitting across from me.

He answered without looking up. "Yeah, they're good kids."

"Too bad they can't date while they're on missions. I would hook one of them up with our son!"

Theo is twenty now. He's ready for a serious girlfriend.

He keeps breaking up and getting back together with this girl from another state, but he only sees her sporadically. That's not very stable.

On the other hand, every missionary girl is smart, beautiful, has some college under her belt, and shares the same faith. I love them all! How awesome would it be to be the mother-in-law of a wonderful girl like that?

Pocket hesitated. "He's not ready for that yet. He's gotta get himself together first."

"Maybe she could help him?" *He's been struggling with his confidence for a while. It shows in the kind of job he chose and his seeming lack of motivation to pursue a college education. Perhaps the right girlfriend could help motivate him - even if it's only to impress her.*

"He probably wouldn't do it anyway. He's really into the girl that he has that long-distance relationship with." Pocket shrugged.

I should be happy that our son is even attending the missionaries' lessons.

Nodding, I went back to scrolling through social media.

• • •

The missionaries called later in the day to teach us about perseverance and keeping the faith when things get tough. *The basic message is that if we pray to Heavenly Father, he listens to us because we are his children, and he loves us.*

They sent a picture saying something simple that made me pause. "His love now surrounds you."

If God's love surrounds us, why can't I stop bad things from happening to me? Better yet, why can't he?

The missionaries didn't have any satisfactory answers to these questions. They said: "Bad things happen to us, but we learn and grow from these experiences" or "Each of us made decisions in the pre-existence...blah blah blah". I can learn and grow without having all those problems in my life.

When I challenged their opinion, instead of doubling down or expanding on it, they invited us to watch the General Conference happening in a few days. It would be streamed worldwide, due to COVID, instead of being held in person.

"What is this General Conference?" I focused on their faces, forgetting to look at the camera.

"The General Conference is like the Super Bowl for the Mormon church.

During it, the President of the entire church worldwide, his two counselors, and other members of the worldwide leadership in the church give speeches to the whole church about church doctrine and Jesus Christ using the Bible and The Book of Mormon. If the President of the church, also known as the Prophet, gets a message from God, that's where he usually says it.

They also have someone give a quick statement about church business and finances so that members know what the church does with all their donation money. It lasts two days, and if you watch every section of it, it's exhausting!

You'll get more out of it if you take notes and write questions you need answers to in a notebook. Listen to the speeches with purpose and get answers to your questions."

• ◦ •

Two days later, Pocket and I sat faithfully in front of the television.

Listening with purpose doesn't guarantee that you'll get answers to all your questions, but it worked for Pocket. He heard everything he wanted to know.

It didn't work for me, but I expected it because my mind is analytical. I know too much about the Bible to have faith just because. Something needs to show me the likelihood that what I'm asked to believe in is possible.

At least I'm taking the lack of answers better than expected. Instead of being angry with God or envious of Pocket, I'm happy for my partner.

"How do you like it so far?" The missionaries texted during one of the breaks.

"It's been great! Lots of info, I can't take notes fast enough." I added the praise hands emoji. *It's true. Whenever I write a thought or a note from someone's speech while they're speaking, by the time I finish, I miss a whole section of the speech and can't rewind because the conference is live.*

I glanced over at Pocket, who slept with his cell phone still on his chest, and shook my head. *He slept through most of it and somehow still got his questions answered.*

"Hahaha, same! The talks should all be published to reread in a few days tho! If one sticks out to me, I note what session it was in and who the speaker is!"

I nodded, even though they couldn't see me.

"That's what I had to do! I'd take notes, and while writing, I'd miss something else. Meanwhile, Pocket kept screaming out 'There's another answer for me!' as if playing biblical bingo and threw me off track."

The hymn music sung before and after every session bugs me though. Neither Pocket nor I are into hymn music. We can't relate. When the church sings every Sunday at sacrament, we stare at the open hymnbook and glance at each other.

Once the General Conference ended, our following lessons came from different speeches that we heard during it.

I'm used to people teaching from the Bible and got used to being taught from The Book Of Mormon, but learning church stuff based on some guys' words that aren't even scripture is just weird. I mean, they aren't Jesus or his disciples. They aren't the apostle Paul.

Every scripture that needs to be written has already been written.

The Bible, The Book of Mormon, the Pearl of Great Price, and Doctrine and Covenants have already been canonized. Why take these speeches as gospel if we already have books with the gospel in them? People could be led away by these guys, following them instead of the scriptures.

I'll take their messages as good advice rather than scripture.

Suddenly, a thought popped into my head. "*You read books and testimonies from people who have learned and developed in the gospel, and you learn from them. This is the same.*"

Okay, God...

• ◦ •

The day after the General Conference, the missionaries sent another message.

"We're talking to an attorney right now, and he said he can check with the court today. He wants to know if it's in our county and if it's a contested divorce, uncontested divorce, or dissolution."

Still nervous about the whole situation, I hesitated. *Do I want the missionaries to continue being the middle-man? I'd feel terrible if they got in trouble for helping me with my divorce.*

"It's in our county. It's uncontested. I filed a complaint for divorce. The defendant disappeared so I completed the six-week notice of publication to no response. And now I just need the court hearing for the decree of divorcement to be signed."

My phone dinged with a response right after.

"He's wondering what your case number is."

I sent the case number, and they promised me they'd find out.

• ◦ •

Finally. Whatever the lawyer did must have worked because the court called in two days after weeks of silence.

"The case management office for the county domestic relations court called. She said they're trying to get things done as quickly as possible and that the lady who schedules the court dates for divorce will be in next week, so I may get a phone call at that time. Pray that I get an early date."

I clutched my phone tightly as if praying.

"We will for sure! When we talked to the attorney, he found out that your case was in the judge's office waiting to be assigned, and that they may give you a phone call hearing, which will make it a lot faster!"

That would be amazing! It looks like I'm on the path to divorce! Once I finalize the divorce, I can get married and baptized.

"They did tell us that for now all April baptisms have been canceled." They added an emoji with exasperated eyes.

"Maybe they'll find a way to make an exception when it's time for baptism?" *I really hope it's possible.*

"There are some exceptions, but we have to get approval first. So fingers crossed."

I want to get divorced as quickly as possible to be ready for an April baptism, and Pocket is looking for his proof of divorce for the same reason. Turns out Pocket's wife already divorced him and that's why he had to give her half of everything he owned. He received a copy of the divorce papers in the mail.

I shook my head.

Pocket hardly ever checks the mailbox. When he does check the mailbox, he tosses his mail on the stairs leading up to our bedroom.

Once he gets tired of seeing it sitting there, he throws it away unopened. If, by some miracle, he does open the mail, he loses it not long after. That's why the best way to contact him is through email.

He's been on a mad search for his divorce documents for a while now. Please, God, help him find them.

9

DIVORCE IMMINENT

"Hey, has your letter come back yet?" Sister Squire and Sister Robison texted.

All this time I waited for a letter from the courts telling me that they received all of the necessary documents needed to schedule a court date for the divorce. And when it finally arrives, I get this.

I texted, fingers trembling. "I got the letter from the courts ... bad news. I got a list of stuff I gotta do to prove that I tried to find my ex for my stuff to go through."

"Oh no, what did they say?"

"I can't deal ... Oh, so much." My heart pounded in my throat.

"You're freaking kidding me." The sisters' reply came quickly.

I'm sure they're dumbfounded. This is probably the first time that these young ones have tried to help a person get divorced.

They probably couldn't believe that after all we did and all the paperwork we turned in, there was still more to do. I can hardly believe it myself. Well, if anything, I hope this teaches them to be picky when they get married so they'll never find themselves in this situation.

"I don't think I'll be able to do it. And if I do find him I don't think it'll be good for me. There's a reason we haven't seen or heard from each other in five years." Teardrops fell on my shirt.

"What else do they expect you to do?"

"I can't do this. It's over. I'm serious." *I can feel a panic attack coming.*

"Well, we know that God isn't going to let this stop you. We'll figure it out. What does the judge want you to do? I'm so triggered."

Me too.

I listed the fourteen items that the judge requested. Depression came creeping in. *I feel defeated, like I got sucked into a black hole of immense sadness.* Tears ran down my face as I started to hyperventilate, and my chest hurt.

"All that to find him. And I have to have proof I did all that stuff for my case to be a final appealable order. I'm never going to get baptized. I just don't have the mental fortitude." Leaning back onto the couch, I put my head in my hands. *I don't want to give up, but what can I do? This is too much.*

"Okay, we're going to get through this. We can help you."

I don't know how such young girls have so much stamina and fortitude to work through this issue with me. None of us know what we're doing.

As the adult in this situation, I should be encouraging them, not the other way around.

"I promise this. Satan is doing this, but we aren't letting him win. Take a deep breath. Don't think about it tonight. Go watch a movie with Pocket and Theo.

We'll get together with Jake, Courtney, the bishop, and other people from the ward. Maybe we could give each person an assignment from the list and knock it out in one day. We can also get you another blessing. You have God's army behind you.

If you weren't a threat to Satan he wouldn't be making it so hard but I PROMISE, as set-apart missionaries of Jesus Christ, you will be baptized."

I feel a little better. Well, as 'better' as one can feel in my situation. I put my phone down. Trying to focus on my breathing, I closed my eyes and wiped the tears off my face.

Perhaps I was reckless. I should have never tried to do my own divorce without a lawyer.

● ∙ ●

The missionaries assigned to my house have tenacity. No matter what happens, how many steps back we take, or the number of pitfalls; they never quit and they always stay positive.

Grabbing a box of instant oats off the top of the fridge, I shook my head.

I'm sure that they never got trained for this in the Missionary Training Center. They must be doing it because they care about us.

In my wildest dreams, I couldn't imagine them learning how to get a mentee of the church or an investigator as they call it, a divorce from an estranged spouse.

When I asked them if they were supposed to be helping this much, they traded smiles, shrugged, and went back to planning our next move.

I filled the oats with milk and put them into the microwave. Setting the timer, I leaned against the counter to wait.

God must have sent them. I can't imagine any other missionaries going through the trouble.

The next day I got a text from them. "We just talked to the attorney and he said we should talk to Brother Edmons in our ward because he's the most qualified attorney for the nature of this case. He also said that you should call the court to let them know that he has been located and ask how they would like you to proceed. I don't know if Brother Edmons can do it for free, but possibly cheaper. What do you think?"

They're right. At this point, two teen missionaries and an inexperienced adult would need more help if we wanted to succeed.

"I like the idea of talking to Brother Edmons. I don't have an address for my ex though so I don't really consider that being located."

"We have the address."

My jaw dropped as shock reverberated through my body. *How did the missionaries find him so fast?*

"Oh, okay. Well then yeah, we need Brother Edmons because I don't know what to do from here." I texted back quickly as if my hands weren't trembling. When they sent over his address I swallowed hard. *Now things were getting real.*

"Okay! We'll email the lawyer right now!" They texted his

contact information a few minutes later. "Cool! So call him at that number like tomorrow and he said he can help!"

I stared at my phone, stunned. *Things are happening so fast. I mean, I wanted it to go quickly, but not if I'd have to see my ex. I can't stand to be in the same room, on the phone, or on Zoom together. We've been through too much and I'm afraid of what he might say or do if we make contact.*

"I'll call first thing in the morning. Thank you so much. (Still physically sick about this process though.)" *I think I just lost my appetite.*

"Well, let us know if there is anything we can do to help. We can bring you a treat." They added a heart emoji.

I smiled.

Everyone in the church sent treats and cards to us as soon as they heard about our efforts to get baptized. Between the side effects from my medication and all the treats I devoured, I gained so much weight. Far from the well-oiled machine that I was when I entered the psych ward.

I'm not happy about the weight gain, but I'm grateful for all the support.

In the middle of the divorce, we got new missionaries, and the old missionaries were sent to a new town.

What on earth is this? What's going on? They told us when we met that they were our friends and we became very close. They're like family and now Sister Robison has to leave to go to a new area. I don't get it, how can they leave like that?

Why would they call us friends if they were just going to abandon us?

Sister Robison came to visit during a COVID break. Sitting on my couch, she leaned over. "Normally missionaries only stay in an area for a certain amount of time and I've been in this area for a long time. Sister Squire will still be here after I go, so it won't be too bad."

Sister Squire smiled and nodded slowly.

I can't believe it. Sister Robison has been with us for at least six months. Maybe that's because when she was about to get transferred we would get a baptism date. Every time something happened to change the date. I really want her to be there for our baptism.

It was bad enough that a few months back, Sister Bullard returned to her home in another state out west because her mission time had ended. I only got through that because I had Sister Robison and we had only known Sister Bullard for a few weeks.

However, Sister Robison leaving is too much!

I prayed to God that night for the first time in a long time. Tears streamed down my face.

Why would you give me a friend and then take her away? My heart feels like it's breaking.

The night was quiet, but later I received a message from her.

"Don't worry, we'll always be friends. I'll add you to my emails. You know, the ones where I give weekly updates about my mission experiences."

All right, it still doesn't feel right, but at least I'm not losing her completely. Her stories are hilarious, and her pictures are cool – except the ones of spiders. She loves spiders and even holds them in her hands. I could never even imagine having a pet tarantula.

Once Sister Robison left, a missionary named Sister Michaelis came to introduce herself. She was a petite girl with smart glasses and strawberry blond, naturally wavy hair.

Hard to imagine her as the only girl of triplets.

Between Sister Robison and Sister Squire, the latter is the shy and quiet one except when she wholeheartedly believes in something and the passion overflows. But this new Sister also seems more introverted.

How is this going to work out if they're both quiet?

Because she had been in the area longer, Sister Squire took the lead. *How surprising. She's doing well though.*

Over time Pocket and I noticed her growth. *I can see her improving as she gains more confidence from mission work with Sister Michaelis. She's now effortlessly stepping into the role of lead missionary.*

Before we knew it, it was time for Sister Squire to transfer to a different place, leaving Sister Michaelis with a new missionary named Sister Doane.

Sister Doane was short and sweet with an infectious smile, sun-kissed brown hair, and bronze skin. Not dark bronze, but light as if she had a perpetual suntan.

Between Zoom meetings with the missionaries, people from the church would come by our house, stand on our front step, and hang out with us. COVID was still around, but the leaders of the church sent out a statement saying that although we couldn't meet inside people's houses, we could meet outside in small groups if each person kept six feet apart.

The missionaries who were locked in their apartments, only

allowed to leave for a limited time to exercise and buy groceries, were released. They also joined us on our front step to give us words of encouragement, share spiritual thoughts, and lift our spirits.

Normally, we don't have that many people who come to visit.

Seeing everyone from the church brightens our day. I'm sure it lifts their spirits as well. Everyone wants to see us succeed. It's so amazing to have so many people cheer you on during a worldwide pandemic, toilet paper shortage, and difficult divorce procedures.

The divorce was still up in the air when Sister Michaelis and Sister Doane became our missionaries.

Sister Squire must have gotten everyone up to speed when they came because everything went smoothly. No hiccups, at all. I didn't have to rehash what we've been doing for this divorce to happen nor relive the nightmare. It's like they just picked up where the previous missionaries left off.

"God will help you make of yourself something greater than you ever thought possible. - Dieter F. Uchtdorf." The missionaries sent a quote from a speech given by one of the worldwide leaders of the church.

Sister Michaelis and Sister Doane kept sending us inspiring texts along with quotes and putting sticky notes with scriptures and words of encouragement on our front door.

Often, I'd leave home only to find colorful sticky notes upon my return. *I should keep these. I'll put a happy wall in my room and stick all these sticky notes on it so I can look at them whenever I'm feeling down.*

Even with my new wall, the divorce still loomed over my head.

I need to focus on something other than the divorce. After all, I don't have any real control over it anyway.

To further help me, the missionaries decided to revisit the Word of Wisdom with Pocket and me. They challenged me to stop drinking coffee for twenty-one days.

That's impossible. I tried to quit coffee before, and it didn't work. "Fine, I'll do it, but only if you give up something too."

Sister Doane smiled. "I'll give up peanut butter. I'm practically addicted to it. Give me a spoon, and I'll eat it right out of the jar. If I give that up, I'll be able to understand what you're going through."

"I'll give up flavored water then." Sister Michaelis smiled as well, rubbing her neck.

I chuckled. "That's not a real sacrifice."

"No really, I don't like regular water. All the water I drink is flavored."

Let's push her a little. "Yeah, but you have to drink water no matter what. Even if you don't like the taste, you need it to live."

"Trust me." She blushed. "It's definitely a sacrifice for me."

• • •

What's this? It's only day one, and you'd think I haven't eaten for weeks! I feel tired and sluggish. The more I try to push myself to do everyday tasks, the weaker I become.

All of this because I didn't have coffee?!

My head throbbed with a mild headache. I wet my face to try to snap out of the fog.

Suddenly, my phone dinged. The missionaries sent a short video of themselves, illustrating their first day of our restrictions. *They look good. Not half alive like I feel. They still have color on their faces and are energetic.*

"Keep going! You're doing a good job." Their cheerful voices echoed.

Butterflies fluttered in my stomach. *I'm so happy they sent me a video.* "Oh my gosh! I love this so much. I'm still going strong. Today was the hardest. There was so much temptation everywhere, but I didn't break." I added a praying hands emoji. "You guys are doing great as well."

• • •

By day three, I had headaches, a runny nose, and cold-like symptoms, but I still got on the Zoom call that night for a lesson.

Sister Doane looked at me and smiled. "How's everything going?"

She probably wants to know how my no-coffee fast is going.

"I'm so sick!" My face flushed, and cold sweat dotted my forehead. "My head hurts, and I feel like I'm going to vomit." *I didn't eat much in the last three days because I felt terrible. I can barely drag myself out of bed in the morning, and I only manage to make it through the day thanks to a long midday nap.*

"Yeah? Maybe you can drink some juice or something that will give you natural energy. It's okay. It'll get better."

"What about you?" I barely looked into the camera.

She nodded and smiled again.

Sister Doane always smiles. I have never seen her without a smile since I've met her. I probably wouldn't even be able to identify her if she walked past me without smiling.

"It's been tough. Very tough, because I love peanut butter, and I usually eat it many times a day … but it's probably not as bad as what you or Sister Michaelis are going through." She nodded her head towards Sister Michaelis.

Sister Michaelis looked jaundiced! Her color was off. She looked weak and a bit disheveled.

My eyes opened wide. "What happened to you?"

"I don't like unflavored water, so I haven't been drinking much…" She smiled weakly.

"Dude! You're gonna kill yourself! You gotta quit the fast." My 'parent voice' came out.

Sister Michaelis shook her head. "No, I can do this. It's just that I don't like unflavored water, so I'm not really drinking any."

I don't even know what to say. "Why did you pick something so important to fast with?"

She shrugged. "I wanted to pick something I knew would be a sacrifice."

I looked at Sister Doane. "Did you know she wasn't drinking water?"

The missionary clasped her hands and looked at Sister Michaelis with a nervous smile.

"You're not allowed to fast anymore. You know that you can die without water, right?" I paused, waiting for an answer.

The girls looked at each other with nervous smiles. "Well…"

"That's it." I cut them off. "You gotta pick something else, Michaelis. I'm sorry, but you can't do this fast." *And that's that.*

If she waits until the fast ends, she'll be dead or in the hospital. No one is dying on my watch.

Sister Michaelis quit the fast, so only Sister Doane and I were left. Since she couldn't participate, she prayed for and encouraged us as we fasted. *That job is hard enough, considering I'm a Debbie Downer without my coffee.*

"Hey, we wanted to follow up and see how your Word of Wisdom goals have been going?" The missionaries kept checking in.

"Well … less coffee. Sometimes no coffee. Been trying to exercise every day, but I'm not consistent. I don't drink tea or herbal tea. I've been sharing the gospel with everyone I know … And I try to eat in moderation, not in boredom." I sat on the couch.

"That's really good! We're proud of you."

It's heartwarming to have their support.

• • •

A little over a week into my coffee fast, I found out that we had finally met the court's requirements for my divorce. Just like that I received a court date near the end of the month. *Yes! We can finally start planning our wedding and baptisms.*

The missionaries jumped on the task swiftly, preparing a guest list that met the church's COVID requirements and discussing who would baptize us and the baptism program.

"Let's have one person do multiple jobs in the program to maximize the seats available for friends and family members. We need two witnesses, and Bishop Ashford can serve as one, we think.

Your son could baptize you (and Pocket if he wanted), or someone else could baptize Pocket (like Jake) then they could confirm you and him and ordain him to the priesthood. The person who confirms you guys can act as the baptism witness. To help give an idea."

The missionaries have thought this through. I shared our list of guests. "The baptism list needs Robison and Squire if they can come."

"Ok, we might be able to have more guests at the wedding if we do it outside. The problem with Sister Robison and Sister Squire is that they have to bring their companions, and we aren't allowed to go to baptisms outside of our areas as missionaries right now. I think the best we can do is to have them on a Zoom call during the wedding."

"Maybe they can switch companions for a day?" I refused to give in. *Sister Robison and Sister Squire did the bulk of the legwork to get me and Pocket to this point. There was no way we would do any of it - marriage or baptism- if they couldn't be there. They worked too hard to not taste the fruits of their labor.*

"Even if they could switch, it's not a great situation. We wish the rules were different too. We don't think we can get around it."

I blinked back tears. "Well ... I dunno what to do. They did so much work to get me here and helped a lot with the court stuff ... I couldn't have done it without them."

Shortly after, I received another message.

"We'll call President later today after meetings and such, and try to find a way."

I sent over the praying hands emoji. *Please, God, let this President guy say yes to my request.*

Over the next few days, we refined the guest list for the wedding and baptism.

Gotta have the wedding before the baptism. Only single or married people can get baptized. The church doesn't condone 'shacking'. Dating and being engaged is okay though, as long as you're not living or sleeping with them. Pocket and I are way past that.

The missionaries forwarded a message between them and Bishop Ashford. "The Bishop said: 'I have thought about possible sites for the wedding. The options would be Jake and Courtney's, my place, or possibly a park. I've reached out to the Guffeys, but haven't heard back yet. Jake and Courtney's yard is more secluded with beautiful greenery if that's the feel they're looking for. Whichever they choose it will be wonderful."

"We'll do it at Jake and Courtney's." *Such an easy decision. Jake and Courtney took us into their family, taught us at BOM club, hosted us at their house when we couldn't go to church due to COVID, and so much more. Every time I get sick, which happens often, Jake gives me a blessing. We love them more than we love pizza! Having our wedding at their house will be a dream come true.*

• • •

As we continued to plan, a couple of weeks passed. During that time, my coffee withdrawal symptoms stopped. *I feel great! My brain is no longer foggy, the constant headache is gone, I have more energy, and my appetite is slowly returning.*

It was during the last few days of the fast that I finally got to sit before a judge for my divorce.

I went to my mother's house for the hearing. *I feel like I'm going to have a heart attack if I have to do it alone. At least, if it doesn't go well, my mom will be there to catch me when I pass out.*

We sat in her living room with her laptop in front of us, waiting on hold for the judge to call my name and case number. In the meantime, I listened to other cases that the judge was ruling on. *She sounds stern. The missionaries told me that she had a background in domestic violence. Hopefully, she'll see all the paperwork explaining my situation and grant me a divorce.*

Suddenly, it was my turn. I swallowed hard, answering identification questions and explaining who else was in the frame. The judge started going through the papers in my file.

"Okay … You are missing…"

After those words, my heart sank, and my mind went blank. *I don't remember what she said after that.*

My mom spoke up. "She turned everything in a few weeks ago. The whole checklist has been completed and should be in the file."

You bet it is. I leaned against my mom. *I'm gonna pass out.*

"Oh, I see. Here it is, right here." The judge pulled out a piece of paper and said some other stuff that I couldn't hear because my heart was beating loudly in my ears, and then it ended. "Divorce granted."

It may be just another day in the office for her, but for me, it's the day of my freedom. I'm finally free! I felt like a huge weight was lifted off my shoulders. I looked at my mom. "I'm glad I did that here because I was about to pass out!" I tried to catch my breath.

Oh, that's right. There's an entire church waiting to find out the results of this court hearing. I grabbed my phone, fingers trembling with excitement, and quickly texted the missionaries.

"DIVORCE GRANTED!"

10

THE ROAD TO BAPTISM

THE MISSIONARIES AND I WENT INTO FULL PLANNING MODE, only stopping to get input from Pocket when we needed it.

Now that I'm divorced, Pocket and I can get a marriage certificate and plan a small wedding and baptism. COVID is still an issue. The church's safety restrictions are even tighter than those of the state.

Honestly, they seem to be very concerned about the safety of their members, so they're more cautious. For example, if the state says groups of 50 could gather indoors and 100 outdoors, as long as each person is six feet apart, the church says that only 20 to 25 people can gather, and only if the gathering is outside. I went over the list, tapping my knee with my pencil.

Because of this, we ended up with three guest lists: one with twenty-two people, one with thirteen people, and one with ten people total. Jumping up from the couch, I headed upstairs to my bedroom.

To get the marriage certificate, Pocket and I need to bring our divorce decrees to the marriage license office as proof that we're legally allowed to marry each other. Thankfully, my decree came rather quickly, and I put it in my travel file for easy access during our appointment with the marriage license office.

On my way to the bedroom, I crossed Pocket crouched on the floor at the bottom of the stairs.

"What's going on?" I watched him quickly dig through the tons of envelopes piled on the stairs. *Pocket isn't good at opening mail, and he normally doesn't care. Why is he opening it all right now?*

"I'm trying to find my divorce decree." Focusing on an envelope, he ripped it open.

My mouth dropped. "What? What are you saying?" I felt that familiar tightening in my chest. "You don't have proof that you're divorced?"

"I know I am. I'm trying to see if I received proof." He continued to open envelopes.

"Are you *sure* you're divorced? You never went to court for anything except child support."

His face flushed so red that even his ears turned red. "I mean, I think I'm divorced even though I didn't go to the hearing. She told me I was."

SHE told you? I struggled to breathe.

'She' means his ex-wife, with whom every conversation he has

is strained. I get that speaking to her is uncomfortable for him. It's uncomfortable even for me sitting in the same room, when they're on the phone together.

I understand why he wouldn't have contacted her for more information or copies of the divorce documents, but that doesn't change the fact that sorting out his paperwork situation was his responsibility.

I tried to take a deep breath while bottling up my anger. "When did you get divorced?"

At this point, he avoided all eye contact with me. "I don't know. I just know that she told me we were divorced…"

'You mean to tell me…" I hissed, steam practically leaking from my ears. "Not only do you NOT have your divorce decree, you don't even know when you got divorced!?" Heat seared through my body. "You had six months to sort this out. The whole time I went back and forth trying to get a divorce, you could have done this." I shook as I controlled myself, then turned around and walked out of the room before I started yelling.

Pocket and I rarely disagree, and we never yell at each other. When we do disagree, my voice gets softer the angrier I get. Pocket announces he's upset and doesn't want to talk, kisses me on the forehead, and leaves to be alone.

I hate being angry like this. Usually, we make up five minutes later, but I need time to calm down.

Just as I left the room, a text from the missionaries came through. "Hey! How are you doing?"

What's with their timing? They always seem to text me when

I need it the most. I'm not sure how they knew that I needed a friend. "Hanging in there." I tried to catch my breath, a minute from full-on panic mode.

"You need to talk?".

"I'll be ok. Just frustrated." While doing breathing exercises, I contemplated if I should dump more adult issues onto the missionaries. I hesitated.

I'm sure that being a missionary shouldn't be as hard as my family and I were making it for them. Every time the sister missionaries help me, along with gratitude I feel an undertone of guilt. They just want to get me and my family baptized, but they have to move mountains to make that happen. It isn't fair to them.

"Are you frustrated with the court?"

Should I respond? I waited a couple of minutes to calm down first. "I'm frustrated with Pocket. He procrastinated so much. He had the full six months that I was going through my divorce to get his paperwork together, and he just recently tried to find it."

"We're so sorry! That's really hard. Are there any updates?" The missionaries were ready to jump in to assist.

• • •

A few hours later, Pocket and I had a proper talk.

"Let's not wait on your divorce decree to make an appointment with the marriage license office to get our license." I sat next to him, putting my hand on his shoulder.

Pocket nodded.

At least we got an appointment quickly. Compared to the rest of our journey so far, this part moves the fastest. I conveyed the information to the Sisters.

"Pocket told me that he called the courts in the small southern town where he and his ex-wife lived and got married. The courthouse clerk said that they can check their records to see if they have the decree that he's searching for on file, but he has to physically come to the courthouse to get it. The small town courthouse is five hours south of where we live, and closes during the weekend.

He'd need to take time off work to drive down, so he took a shot in the dark and asked them if it was possible to have the document emailed to him if they found it. They agreed." I smiled.

"If he hasn't received the email with his decree yet, make sure Pocket follows up with the courthouse the next day before they close."

"Okay. So Pocket finally got a date for our marriage license. September 22 at 11:30am. He said we can now firmly set September 26th as the wedding date." Giggling with excitement, I let out a squeal of happiness.

"YAY! That's so exciting. This might call for a celebration treat!"

We're finally making headway. Pocket and I feel more excited about our baptism than our wedding.

Having a wedding ceremony is great, but in all honesty, it wouldn't change our relationship with each other. It was just a piece of paper needed to join the church. We had been together so long that we already felt married. We both loved each other unconditionally, so a ceremony wasn't necessary. Whatever we had to do we wanted it done by September 26th.

"Bishop Ashford has to work on September 26th, and the weekend after is the General Conference."

Again? It seems like every time we get close to being baptized members of the church some obstacle would push the date back.

I explained things to the missionaries.

"So you want to push the date back to wait for Bishop to be available?" The Sisters replied fast, as always.

"He pushed the date back. We kinda need him. He said he's available on the 10th of October. He also said that it'll give us time in case we run into trouble with the license. (Like if they mail it instead of handing it to us)." I rummaged through the fridge looking for something soothing to eat. *God forbid it gets lost in the mail.*

"Very true! You all are awesome! We love you and can't wait."

• • •

Pocket seems to be more proactive than before. He finally received his divorce decree via email. Time passed like a whirlwind. Not long after, we stood outside the courthouse with huge smiles, taking selfies of us holding our new marriage certificate.

However, COVID continued to wreak havoc on our wedding attendee list.

It's down to ten now. That's the final number we're working with. That leaves us with Jake and Courtney, because it's their house, and they're our friends, plus Courtney's a photographer.

We needed Bishop Ashford because he'll be performing the ceremony. My mom, Pocket's mom, our daughter Jo, our son Theo, and my sister Apriel are also invited. I counted the names on the wedding list.

We can't tell Jo there's a wedding though. Jo, like Pocket, can't keep secrets when she's excited. Pocket and his ex-wife share custody, but she spends a lot of time with her mom. If she says anything about the wedding while she's still there, her mom might not let her come. I put a star next to her name.

We already don't get to see Jo a lot, so it's always a big deal when she comes. Sometimes her mom tries to get her to come home early causing an argument, and she ends up crying in her room for the rest of her stay. I rubbed my forehead.

Jo is a sweet, sensitive, beautiful girl with impeccable style, and she loves to keep up with the newest hair trends. Her makeup is usually immaculate, always perfectly matching her outfit.

She'll probably be a bit upset that she won't be able to plan her outfit, but she'll get over it since it's not what's most important. That way, no one can make her cry or do anything that would turn it into a sad day for her. Or worse, force Pocket to bring her back south five hours away on our wedding day. Staring at my guest list, I sighed and leaned back on the couch.

Pocket really isn't good at keeping secrets.

During a conversation with Jo, he let it slip twice that we were getting married, but luckily, she didn't catch it.

Me, Theo, and my eight-year-old niece, Janelle - who also knew and was sworn to secrecy - looked at him with raised eyebrows. Jo didn't notice, though.

I discussed it with Pocket, who agreed. *It's better to tell her the day before the wedding instead of the day of the wedding, as planned.*

We sat her down for a talk.

"Oh! Why didn't you tell me? I was going to pack a dressy white shirt, but I looked at it like 'When would I ever use this?' and I didn't." Jo practically bounced on her chair.

We laughed.

I'm glad we don't have to keep the secret any longer. "We didn't want anyone to find out and keep you from coming."

"Oh no! There would be no way anyone would have kept me from this - we'd be going at it!" She nodded, crossing her arms.

"Well, we didn't want you to have to do all that and figured you'd want to be here for your dad. Now, if anyone finds out you went to the wedding, you can honestly say that you didn't know about it until the day before." I winked.

That night, we all hung out in the living room together, telling stories and reminiscing.

At least there's one good thing about COVID. Normally the kids and I often spend a lot of time together, whereas Pocket is at work, and is tired when he comes home, so he only gets to hang out a little bit before he has to go to bed. Now Pocket has more time to hang out with all of us.

Like kids on Christmas Eve, we all went to bed excited, looking forward to the next day.

● ● ●

As I put on the gold curb chain bracelet given to me by Pocket's mom to wear for our wedding day, I caught a glimpse of myself in the mirror. Its matching necklace caressed my collarbone delicately.

I took a minute to take in my total look. My off-white empire waist floor-length dress was simple with only a twinkling of gold on the seam of the empire waist. I didn't have a veil to wear.

This dress only cost twenty dollars from a local store, but it definitely didn't belong there. It looked like it should cost at least a hundred dollars at a name-brand store.

It's a gift from Heavenly Father for my special day.

I slept on hard curling mesh rods, so my scalp ached as I pulled each roller out of my hair. *I don't care. My makeup is camera-ready, and that delicate gold tiara will look amazing in these soft curls.*

"Babes, can you help me with this bracelet?" I walked into our room. *These ballerina slippers make me feel shorter than usual, or maybe it's because Pocket has dress shoes on, making him seem taller.*

I stopped for a moment. *Pocket looks great.*

He wore a tailored royal blue suit, white shirt, and blue tie. His red beard contrasted with his blue suit, and I could smell his soft yet rugged cologne. *It makes me want to get lost in one of his soothing hugs. I won't reach for him, though, because I don't want to smell like him at the wedding. I want to smell delicate and sweet.*

"It's kinda small compared to my wrist."

"Nope." The clasp on the bracelet clicked shut. "It's just fine."

Our eyes met, the specs of brown and green in his hazel eyes enhanced by his haircut and trimmed beard. I lowered my eyes, blushing. *He looks amazing. I've never seen Pocket so cleaned up. He dresses nicely on Sundays at sacrament, but not to this extent. I almost didn't recognize him.*

I looked at my phone, breaking the tension. "Well, It looks like it's time to get going." I grabbed the matching sheer, off-white, shawl off of the bed. *If I wear it over my head with the tiara, I'll look like a woman from Jesus' day, and for some reason, I love the look.*

Pocket's mom lent us her Silver T-Top Firebird, a collectors' item, to ride to the wedding. The engine roared as Pocket started the car, announcing its muscle. He opened the top. *Surprisingly, I don't even care that I suffered through the night to have curls in my hair as the wind running through my curls feels delightful.*

Lost in the moment, Pocket gave the car more gas, and the engine rumbled. Its racing tires floated over the pavement.

"You better be careful with your mom's car. You know how it can get away from you." I fidgeted in my seat. "A car with this type of tires would run better on a racetrack than a regular road." *Before, when we took the car to the shop for its usual maintenance, Pocket did a hook-slide as he entered the highway. I was terrified that he would crash his mom's pride and joy and worried about how we would explain what happened. Thankfully, he regained control of the car and merged into traffic. I don't need anything like that on our wedding day.*

We pulled into Jake and Courtney's driveway carefully and parked in front of their garage.

Following the walkway on the side of the house, surrounded by trees, the small path opened up to reveal their backyard decorated with beautiful white cloth-covered chairs with purple satin bows. To the left was their wooden outdoor deck with a table draped in white cloth, filled with delicious sweets, treats, pulled pork and buns, and beautifully staged finger sandwiches.

Each had a small white card, embroidered with gold and the names of the people from the church who donated the item.

Our kids arrived as Pocket and I were taking pre-wedding photos near the trees further in the yard.

Theo wore a three-piece black suit with a black and white vertical pinstripe vest, and Jo wore an open-shoulder black top with a purple, black, and white plaid miniskirt. *Somehow all of us ended up matching the wedding colors even though we never discussed them.*

Of the mothers, Pocket's mom arrived first, dressed casually in a pair of smart blue slacks and a beautiful blouse with small flowers on it. She brought a thin sweater to toss over her shoulders in case it got cold. After all, it was October. Since she was early, Pocket and I got to take some pictures alone with her.

As we were taking photos my mom entered wearing a floor-length black gown with a gold and emerald crystal necklace, which I bought for her birthday a few years ago.

I greeted and hugged her. "You look nice." A smile tickled my lips. *It has been a long time since I saw my mom dressed up. I can see how delighted she is.*

She laughed daintily. "Thanks for the compliment."

Motioning toward the seating area, I moved over. "You can grab a seat if you like."

Theo escorted her to one of the carefully decorated chairs.

As the ceremony would soon start, Bishop Ashford called us into Jake and Courtney's house for a quick rundown of the ceremony, to go over our vows, and answer any questions that we may have. We didn't have many questions so after the meeting we all took our places.

Courtney's a real photographer so she would be taking pictures during the ceremony. Jake would stream on Zoom so that members of the church could attend virtually, and our son would stream on a private social media platform so that our followers could attend.

However, time was ticking, and my sister still hadn't arrived. *I told her it was an hour earlier than the actual ceremony because she usually comes late, but she's still not here. She should have been a Hollywood star because she always looks top-tier when she goes out. Then again, what's the point of arriving camera-ready if you miss the event?*

Pocket and I stood on the deck, in front of the food table, our arms entwined, waiting for her to arrive.

I called her moments before stepping into my place next to Pocket on the deck, and she told me she was en route. It sounded like she was near, so I convinced everyone to give her more time to arrive. I leaned against Pocket, tired of standing.

C'mon Apriel, I can't hold people much longer. I pleaded in my head, hoping that she could feel the urgency in my heart. Pocket and I exchanged looks. Smiling nervously I looked into his eyes. "Just a few more minutes, please."

After ten minutes, Pocket was ready to begin. Everyone on social media and Zoom waited for the wedding to start. I squirmed, begging silently. *Maybe she'll show up in the middle of the ceremony. I want her to be here because we're close. Please don't miss it.*

"Nobody sits around and waits for a guest to arrive." Pocket's calm voice broke me out of my thoughts. "You're the bride. You don't postpone your wedding for a guest, this is about you." He made a good point. *Plus we're on a schedule since the baptism is after the wedding.*

I looked at him. *I felt torn. He was right, though. If this was a large normal wedding, I wouldn't wait. I wouldn't even know if a person didn't come, so it would just go on as planned. However, this was a tiny wedding. Every person counted, and every spot on the guest list taken was one that someone else wanted.*

Before I could make a decision, he turned to the tiny audience. "Let's get started."

"Are you sure?" Bishop Ashford looked at me. "We can wait a little longer. I know you really want her here."

My mother turned in her seat to make eye contact, giving me the 'wrap it up' signal with her finger.

I nodded. "Let's go."

The Bishop agreed, and the ceremony began. I dragged my feet along the grass, stalling for time while trying to make it look like I was walking at a regular pace, to take my place in front of the Bishop. Sneaking a glance at the deck and the path one last time to see if she would walk out, I turned to face Pocket.

The wedding ceremony took all of eight minutes to complete because we didn't have any music and no one gave any speeches.

We went straight into the part where the Bishop talks about

how important marriage is and gives us marriage advice. I suppose that was sort of a speech, but I didn't hear much of it. I stared at the knot on Pocket's tie, which was at eye level. *This is taking a long time.*

I glanced up at Pocket, noticed he was looking at me, and went back to staring at his tie. *I don't know why I'm so nervous. This changes nothing. He's still going to be the same guy when this is over.*

"...time and all eternity?" The Bishop asked.

That's a long time. I swallowed hard. "I will, I do." *...I don't know about eternity... The last time I got married it felt like I was going to have a full-on panic attack. It was so bad that I barely made it through the vows without the Minister stopping the ceremony to do breathing exercises with me. This feels similar, though less severe.*

I want to be married to Pocket, I'm just afraid that he'll change after we get married like the last guy did.

Before I knew it, the Bishop finished his speech and moved on to the part where we said our vows. *I'm so nervous that I don't even remember what I agreed to. All I can think about is that we'll have to kiss in front of everyone, including our kids. It better be a respectful kiss. I told him not to give me a super sexual one. He swore he wouldn't, but he had that devilish twinkle in his eye. Who knows what he's up to?*

The Bishop told us that we could kiss. Pocket leaned in and gave me the sweetest, most respectful, and un-embarrassing kiss that made my heart flutter with happiness. I smiled. *Yes! I made it without having a panic attack.*

Turning to face the audience, the Bishop announced us husband and wife to our loved ones, who cheered happily.

Jo threw her arms around me. "You're my real stepmom now - watch out." We posed for a photo. *Rather than step or whatnot, you're just my daughter. You and Theo are both my kids.*

We ran over to the Zoom callers and social media stream watchers to thank them for attending our wedding virtually and read their comments. We were so focused on the phone screens that we didn't notice my sister enter the backyard from the deck.

I feel like I should turn around. My sister stood there dressed in an emerald-colored babydoll dress that clung to her voluptuous frame and heels. The heels made her 5"11 frame appear 6"2. She was gorgeous!

I scurried up the steps quickly and wrapped her into an embrace. "Awww! You missed it..." I whined with an exaggerated sad face.

"I did?" She looked around at the few guests mingling with each other.

"It was really fast. It only took about five minutes, and then it was over."

"Oh." She dropped her arms, slapping her sides.

Apriel looks both surprised and disappointed. "Stay around for the reception." I pointed to the table full of food and treats.

She nodded, admiring the spread. "This looks great! Who put this together?"

"Jake and Courtney. People from the church also donated different things." I beamed.

"Oh, I brought you something." She smiled coyly.

Please let it be cheesecake. I crossed my fingers. *No wonder my sister's cheesecake business is a success. She makes the best cheesecake I've ever tasted. Whenever she comes, I ask her to make a cheesecake or bring a slice for me. My whole household is addicted.*

She stepped aside to reveal two of her famous cheesecakes.

"Yes!" I pushed past her. *There are two! I got both a peach and brownie turtle cheesecake. They look splendid on the table with the other food.* I looked for something to cut it with to get the first taste. Its velvety smoothness melted on my tongue. "So good." I stuffed my mouth.

● ● ●

Moving into the sunroom with our plates of food, all of the guests made polite conversation. My heart pounded loudly in my ears. *Both of our parents are in the same room together, and my mom will meet my friends. What if they don't get along? What do I do?* I felt the familiar feeling of anxiousness creep back in. *I loathe that feeling you get when people are being polite, but an onlooker can tell that the vibe is off. Even when we take pictures, I'm hyper-aware of that behavior.*

Since the baptism would take place a couple of hours after the reception, someone suggested we go home, change clothes, and rest. Exhaustion overtook my body from the ceremony and my hypervigilance. *Rest sounds like a wonderful idea.*

● ● ●

A few hours later, Pocket and I pulled up to the church in his mom's T-Top Firebird, with the top still down, amongst a small crowd of church members waiting to be let into the church. Pocket still wore his suit, but I had changed into jeans and a comfortable shirt. *We're getting baptized in different clothes anyway. As long as I wear white undergarments, who cares what I wear to the church?*

When we entered the church we saw Sister Robison and Sister Squire. *They made it! Normally, an investigator's current missionaries attend the baptism, but since Sister Robison and Sister Squire did all of the legwork to get to this point, I wanted them to be the ones at our baptism. Luckily, Sister Michaelis and Sister Doane understood and weren't offended. They even helped us make it happen.*

Filled with excitement, we hugged each other.

It feels like it's been forever since I've seen them. Bishop Ashford couldn't be at the baptism because we could only have ten people. That leaves Pocket and me, Jo and Theo, our pianist Brother Hoggart, our speaker Brother Smethers, Jake, who'll be baptizing us, and Pocket's mom - but something happened during the break, so she can't come.

Pocket and I have been trying to get to this moment for months. For so long, it seemed unreachable, and now that it arrived, I don't know what to do with myself.

I gazed at Pocket in the wings of the baptismal font across from me. He and I wore matching white jumpsuits.

We look like painters. For as long as I knew him, Pocket considered himself an atheist. He experienced going to church on holidays, but for the most part, he bounced between not knowing if there was a God and assuming that God didn't exist. When I met him, he knew there was something out there, but he couldn't guarantee it was a God.

Some people say that atheists and agnostics don't have a moral compass and that if a person doesn't believe in Jesus Christ, they won't make a good partner.

My life experience taught me differently. During my dating years, I dated men professing to be Christian and to love Jesus Christ, who were physically abusive, cheaters, manipulators, or just plain mean. I've been married to a narcissist who went to church every Sunday and held positions in the church. He was worse than any unbeliever I've ever met.

When Pocket came along, Jesus Christ was the furthest thing from his mind, and I liked that about him. The exact opposite of any man I'd known, he was genuine, caring, never yelled, and never tried to physically abuse me. I felt emotionally and physically safe with him.

Seeing him step into the water with Jake to get baptized almost brings me to tears.

I stood in the wings, careful not to lean too far into the baptism font. He positioned himself to be dunked in the crystal water. I watched him go under. *The same guy that I loved so much before he went into the water now rose from the water as a man with an unquenchable thirst for Jesus Christ.*

● ● ●

As Pocket made his way back to the wings, he turned to give me a nod of approval and positioned himself, cold and wet, to watch me go under the water. Jake turned to me in the water, smiling reassuringly, his arm extended to help me down the stairs. As our hands clasped together, I gingerly waded into the cold water.

Ahhhh! I fought back a squeal. *The water is freezing!*

Helping me get into a position that would keep me from drowning, Jake spoke the baptism proclamation for all in the room to hear. I paused as I heard my name being called, with my married last name attached to it.

Oh, yeah... I'm married. ...Pay attention! I focused on my breathing, not wanting to be exhaling when going underwater.

"...Father, Son, and Holy Ghost." He dunked me into the freezing water with extreme force, knocking the breath out of me. I screamed as the shock of the freezing water hit me all at once, continuing to scream underwater, and when I broke through the water's surface. *Stop screaming before people think you're possessed by a demon.*

Momentarily confused, I didn't know which way to go to get out of the water. Quietly laughing at my internal monologue, I looked towards the wings to see if Pocket was looking.

He watched silently, waiting for me to exit the water safely.

My eyes focused on Jake, ensuring I got out of the baptismal font without further incident. I went to the dressing room to take off the wet outfit and put my real clothes back on.

As I peeled my jumpsuit off me, the magnitude of what had just happened to Pocket and me hit like a tsunami, causing tears to stream down my face.

Heavenly Father, thank you for getting us to this point.

Feeling pressured by the fact that a small group of people waited for us to join the rest of the baptismal service crowd, I dried hastily and examined my face in the mirror to ensure that there was no evidence of tears. Then I jogged down the hall back to the baptismal room.

Pocket and I agreed that, since we would both be getting a blessing for the Holy Spirit after the baptism, I'd go first.

"I went first the first time, so now it's your turn. That way, if they bless you and 'you begin to melt', I have time to get away." *I wish we were joking, but we're serious. Those church blessings weren't to be given by novices. People's lives were at stake!*

I sat cautiously in the chair positioned in front of the room.

It was placed in a spot where everyone could see what was happening. *They said that I'll receive the Holy Spirit when they begin to bless me.* I gave them my consent to put their hands on my head and closed my eyes. Someone called me by my new full name and spoke a blessing over me. *I can't remember what was said, but I feel like my dot - the one the sister missionaries showed me when they first came to my house - matters. Heavenly Father knows who I am, and he actually loves me and has great plans for me.* I looked at Pocket smiling, signaling him that everything was okay.

They did the same to him, laying their hands on his head. I fought back tears again. *If I cry now, it's going to be loud and ugly. It will be the uncontrollable cries that cause you to hiccup because I've held back tears all day.*

They pronounced that Pocket should receive the Holy Spirit, and by faith he did.

This guy, previously an atheist, had a complete change of heart. All of this happened because two sister missionaries from The Church Of Jesus Christ Of Latter-Day Saints prayed to Heavenly Father about whose house they should visit, received a revelation of our house, and followed the prompting of the Holy Spirit to let me know that my dot mattered to them and Heavenly Father.

They never gave up on us or their missions. I watched Pocket stand and shake the hands that gave him a blessing.

Because of them, Pocket had, at that moment, been affirmed of all the things Heavenly Father knew he was inside. He is blessed, favored by Heavenly Father, and an example to the community. He is a man of wisdom and strength and a man of Jesus Christ.

I'll always love our missionaries for their obedience to the Lord and for their sacrifice.

In the name of Jesus Christ. Amen.

ACCESS YOUR FREE GIFT!

As a huge thank you for supporting my book, I have a GIFT for you. To access it:

- Leave an unbiased review of my book either on Amazon or Goodreads.

- Go to <u>www.mydotmatters.com</u> and fill out the free gift form with your review information.

- Your gift will be delivered to your email's inbox!

XOXO Meka

ABOUT THE AUTHOR

Meka Reed is an award-winning actress and writer in Hollywood films. Born in Cincinnati, Ohio, and raised between Cincinnati and Hyattsville, Maryland, Meka volunteers as the Secretary in the Young Woman's Stake Presidency of the Cincinnati North Stake in The Church of Jesus Christ of Latter-Day Saints. If she isn't spending time with her husband, children, family, friends, and dog, Jada, you can find her writing songs and short stories, binging on true-crime shows, and acting and directing in Hollywood's newest film projects and TV commercials.

www.ingramcontent.com/pod-product-compliance
Lightning Source LLC
Chambersburg PA
CBHW060318050426
42449CB00011B/2534